Anglican Manifesto

Anglican Manifesto

A Christian Response to Oneworld Religion

Jack Estes

WIPF & STOCK · Eugene, Oregon

ANGLICAN MANIFESTO
A Christian Response to Oneworld Religion

Copyright © 2014 Jack Estes. All rights reserved. Except for brief quotations in critical publications or reviews, no part of this book may be reproduced in any manner without prior written permission from the publisher. Write: Permissions, Wipf and Stock Publishers, 199 W. 8th Ave., Suite 3, Eugene, OR 97401.

Wipf & Stock
An Imprint of Wipf and Stock Publishers
199 W. 8th Ave., Suite 3
Eugene, OR 97401

www.wipfandstock.com

ISBN 13: 978-1-62564-441-1

Manufactured in the U.S.A.

All Scripture quotations, unless otherwise indicated, are taken from the The Holy Bible, English Standard Version® (ESV®) Copyright © 2001 by Crossway, a publishing ministry of Good News Publishers. All rights reserved.

Dedicated to my loving wife,
Jenny
With thanksgiving for her faithful support
and encouragement along the way

Contents

List of Illustrations | *viii*
Foreword by Jack Estes | *xi*
Acknowledgments | *xiii*
Thesis | *xv*
Introduction | *xvii*

1 Anglican-Ism | 1
2 Paradigm to Paradigm | 27
3 Two Visions | 49
4 Crisis | 71
5 Anglican Manifesto | 87
6 The Sacramental Principle | 103
7 Oneworld Era | 133

Appendices

1 The Chicago-Lambeth Quadrilateral 1886, 1888 | 157
2 Anglican-Ism Terms and Characters | 160
3 Spiritual Pride | 165
4 Symbols of Oneworld Religion | 167

Bibliography | *171*

Illustrations

0.1 *Ink and quill*; ClipartOf.com/1157541COLLCO178 | xiv
0.2 *Celtic cross*; © Sergey Galushko / Dreamstime.com | xiv
1.1 *Compass rose* | 1
1.2 *Via Media*; © Jack Estes | 6
1.3 © Jack Estes | 24
2.1 *Past, Present, Future*; © Richard Thomas / Dreamstime.com | 27
2.2 © Jack Estes | 31
2.3 *Premodern, Modern, Postmodern*; © Mel Chua, http://blog.melchua.com/2014/05/16/postmodernism-in-a-3-panel-comic/ | 36
2.4 *Scientific Cartoon—In the middle ages*; www.cartoonstock.com (shm1153) | 41
3.1 *Two visions*; © iStock.com/skodonnell | 49
4.1 *Frayed rope*; © iStock.com/DNY59 | 71
5.1 *Haystack*; © Lilittas1 / Dreamstime.com | 87
6.1 *Renaissance Man*; © Cosmin-Constantin Sava / Dreamstime.com | 103
6.2 © Jack Estes | 113
6.3 © Jack Estes | 113
6.4 © Jack Estes | 113
6.5 © Jack Estes | 114
6.6 © Jack Estes | 114
6.7 © Jack Estes | 114
6.8 © Jack Estes | 115
6.9 © Jack Estes | 118
6.10 © Jack Estes | 120
6.11 © Jack Estes | 121

Illustrations

6.12 © Jack Estes | 122
6.13 © Jack Estes | 123
6.14 © Jack Estes | 126
6.15 © Jack Estes | 128
6.16 © Jack Estes | 130
7.1   *Planet earth*; © iStock.com/alexsi | 133
7.2   *One World Trade Tower*; © Bojan Bokic / Dreamstime.com | 138
7.3   *Circle religions*; © Casejustin / Dreamstime.com | 145
7.4   © Jack Estes | 147
7.5   © Jack Estes | 149
7.6   © Jack Estes | 150
7.7   © Jack Estes | 151
8.1   *Comparison of views*; © Pastor Larry Kirkpatrick; OrdinationTruth.com | 167
8.2   *Circle religions*; © Casejustin / Dreamstime.com | 168
8.3   *All World Religion*; © Wai H. Tsang; www.iawwai.com | 168
8.4   *Golden Rule*; © Paul McKenna; Scarboro Missions; www.scarboromissions.ca | 170

Foreword

Dear Reader,

Thank you for your interest in *Anglican Manifesto*. Certainly, we are living through a very dynamic time in the history of the Anglican Church and the world in general. The thesis which follows are my thoughts on how we as Anglicans, and as Christians, can engage with the current situation that we find ourselves in and lay a new foundation for the future.

The Rev. Jack Estes
St. Luke's Anglican Church
2730 Mall View Rd. Bakersfield, CA 93386
stlukesbakersfield@att.net

Acknowledgments

THROUGHOUT THESE PAST SEASONS as I have been working on *Anglican Manifesto*, I have discovered a truth. There is much more to publishing a book than simply writing it. The process begins as an idea, which then grows into a vision. In order to bring the vision into being, writing is just the first stage. Next, comes the rewriting, editing, honing, that in the end results in a book actually becoming a book.

As a writer, I wish to humbly give thanks to those who have patiently assisted me with this process. These are my family, friends, and colleagues who brought their gifts and energy alongside me in order to complete the task:

Jenny Estes
Editing of word choice and reflections on spiritual content

Janelle Eastridge
Editing in grammar, punctuation and plot flow

Shirley Hessler
Computer expertise: illustrations, webpage and Facebook

The Congregation of St. Luke's Anglican Church, Bakersfield, California
Steadfast encouragement and prayer

Thank you to all above. It is my hope that you will share in the fulfillment of God's purposes for this manuscript. I pray God will bless you in bringing your own visions into being as well.

It is not real until it is written
—FR. JACK ESTES

Thesis

The Anglican Communion is uniquely poised to proclaim the gospel to the postmodern culture and expand the kingdom of God in the twenty-first century. In order to effect this proclamation, the immediate crisis of vision, structure, and leadership must be acknowledged and overcome. Essentially, a reformation is needed which provides for a fresh commitment to biblical truth and practice, while uniting Anglicans in common purpose and polity.

Anglican Manifesto examines the underlying principles of the Anglican expression of Christian faith, and how they have interacted with the historical paradigm shifts of, first, Western society, and, now, the global village. Taken together with an analysis of the theological dynamics of the present crisis, *Manifesto* continues with a number of proposals intended to encourage the communion forward into a place of vibrant worship and witness throughout the world. This thesis moves on to propose that the process of Anglican revival become a catalyst for the unification of Christendom in the emerging Oneworld era[1]—the historical paradigm in which we now live.

---

1. So named by the author to describe the next paradigm shift which is already upon us.

Manifesto:
A statement of beliefs and principles with the intention of inciting action
—*MERRIAM-WEBSTER*

Introduction

THE ANGLICAN COMMUNION IS at a crossroads. We have reached the tipping point on the fulcrum, where things can no longer be kept in balance. The decisions made now will effect not only the future direction of Anglicanism, but also the very foundations of Anglican belief. A choice must be made between two competing worldviews, which are at heart radically different. Which foundation shall we chose to build upon? What will the faith of future Anglicans look like? Will there even be an Anglican Church, or will the whole thing simply unravel?

The cataclysmic events now taking place in the Anglican Communion represent a microcosm in the state of Christianity as a whole. The same dynamics which fuel the fires of the current Anglican angst smolder beneath the surface of worldwide Christianity as we move into the twenty-first century. The church universal is facing a polarization between the traditional Christian faith and a revised, progressive "Christianity" that is in fact nothing short of a new religious movement. Christians of every denomination must chose between the two. The foundational principles and theology of each are radically different. They cannot be reconciled: traditional vs. progressive; liberal vs. orthodox; old vs. new; however one makes the distinction we have come to a point of decision.

The time has come for all who would call themselves Christians, to decide which set of beliefs and practices will be adhered to and taught in the church, and which vision will be offered to the world as the Christian faith. Are we sinners brought back into relationship with God through the atoning sacrifice of Jesus Christ, or, are all made in the image of God and therefore inherently good? Is Jesus Christ the only means of salvation, or, is salvation available through a plurality of religions that lead us to the knowledge of the divine presence within each person?

Introduction

While living in and through this historical context, much of the Christian church retains a commitment to the faith once delivered to the saints. Across denominational lines, the "orthodox" hold fast to the belief in an objective authority of the Bible, the transcendent nature of God, and the need for regeneration of sinful human nature. Rather than being informed by the prevailing winds of postmodernity and the directives of liberal theology, many Anglicans, Catholics, and Protestants continue to teach and confess the traditional principles and theology which have been the bedrock of the faith for two thousand years.

Writing from the midst of the struggles of the Anglican Communion, I seek to ignite not only a reformation of Anglicanism, but a global reunification and revival of the Christian church. In the crisis of Anglicanism, I see a historic opportunity for Christianity as a whole. As the tapestry that was once the Anglican Church unravels, I see the possibilities of the bonding together of a new, unified, fellowship of the Christian church worldwide.

Yet, I must confess to a sense of urgency, as the shift to a new era has already begun. We must act, and act soon, or it may well be too late.

And so I give you *Anglican Manifesto*.

Fr. Jack Estes

Ism:
A distinctive doctrine, cause, or theory;
The adherence to a system or class of principles
—MERRIAM-WEBSTER

Chapter 1
Anglican-Ism

THE ANGLICAN CHURCH IS a worldwide phenomena, with thirty-nine provinces spanning the globe, hundreds of bishops and archbishops, and millions of faithful members. As far as Christian denominations are concerned, the Anglican Communion ranks third in strength worldwide, eclipsed only by the Eastern Orthodox Churches and the mammoth Roman Catholic Church led by the pope in Rome. Yet, what exactly is the Anglican-Ism? Ask the question to a room full of Anglicans, and you will probably hear a room full of answers. Ask the question to those outside the Anglican fold, and you may not find any answer that is coherent. To quote a phrase, it's complicated. The answer lies in considering the essential principles on which the Anglican Church was founded to begin with, along with the ongoing historical developments and decisions which have added to its character. Of course, such an undertaking could easily fill several volumes, and what I offer here is more of an astute, succinct assessment for the purpose of this book. Nevertheless, let us consider the following as pieces to the puzzle from which, when properly fit together, emerge a portrait of the Anglican-Ism:

The Church of England

Protestant and Catholic Spirituality

The Via Media

Early Apologists

—Jewel and Hooker

Anglican Comprehensiveness

—The Evangelical Revival and the Oxford Movement

Autonomous Fellowship

Chicago-Lambeth Quadrilateral

The Big Tent

Church of England

The Anglican Reformation—Sixteenth Century

In order to arrive at a coherent discussion of the Anglican reformation of the present day, we must first begin with a consideration of the Anglican Reformation of the sixteenth century—a reformation that was in and of itself part of the larger Protestant movement of the time. For it was in this period of time that foundational principles were established in the Anglican-Ism which continue to exert influence down through time and into the present. For our purposes we will not attempt an exhaustive analysis of the Protestant Reformation. However, certain key elements that formed the distinctively Anglican expression are necessary to identify and explore, so that when we arrive at the discussion of present-day reformation we may understand the theological and ecclesiological landscape in which we live. Specifically, then, let us consider: the conflict between Protestant and Catholic spirituality; the solution of the Via Media; apologists Jewel and Hooker; and the Anglican comprehensiveness that developed as a result.

Protestant and Catholic Spirituality

Spirituality in the broad sense of the word may be best understood as our whole approach to relationship with God. In this sense spirituality includes theology, the understanding of who God is, worship, both corporate and private, revelation, how God communicates, and especially authority, that is what we deem to be authoritative in our spiritual lives. In the sixteenth century, theology, worship, revelation, and authority combined to form the matrix of the conflict between Protestant and Catholic factions within the church: each assumed different approaches to spirituality; each answered the questions of God, man, and church on the basis of their own understanding of authority; and each lived out their own expression of worship as a result.

Catholic spirituality may be viewed as the progressive faction of the day. The Roman Catholic Church could point back through apostolic succession to the Apostle Peter as the first pope of Rome. Thus it was "the" institution of worship in Western society, and as such sought to maintain its position as final arbiter between man and God regarding all things spiritual; tradition, the ongoing life and practice of the church, was viewed as being equally authoritative as Scripture. Both were deemed to be sources of revelation from God: Scripture being the original record of the words and works of God given to mankind; tradition being the progressive ongoing revelation given through the church, as history continued to unfold. While tradition and Scripture ideally would never contradict, in practice one or the other would have to take precedent as final authority in the life of the church. Catholic spirituality of the medieval era chose tradition.

The Catholic spirituality of the time may be best thought of as an outside-to-inside approach to relationship with God. Worship consisted of the external actions and practices of going to mass, confession, penance, giving of alms, etc. In the more advanced monastic forms, praying the daily office, vows of poverty, chastity, and obedience, along with surrender of personal choices in favor of communal life, amplified the understanding that a man's spirit within was conditioned to be closer to God through discipline from without. The external actions and disciplines comprised the spiritual life. Through them the interior of the human heart and spirit were conditioned and transformed, outside to inside.

Protestants were the de facto conservatives of the day, reaching back to the roots of Christianity in the Greek New Testament and apostolic teaching. They sought to correct the church and society from a tradition which they viewed as having erred from God's original revelation in Holy Scripture. *Sola Scriptura*, "Scripture alone," was the rallying cry of the Protestant Reformation. Scripture alone was to be the final authority in all matters regarding both spirituality and church. In order for the church to maintain a proper course down through history, tradition must yield to Scripture, and wherever necessary be corrected by Scripture. Naturally, this did not go over well with those who held the reigns of power in the Roman Church.

The proponents of Protestant spirituality took the opposite approach to their Catholic counterparts. Instead of transforming the human spirit within by means of external actions, it was only God's grace, and faith in him alone, that could redeem and transform the inner man—*sola fide*, "faith alone," and *sola gratia*, "grace alone," were added to form a triumvirate of theological belief. At best, external actions may only offer evidence of a preceding internal transformation. Works were dead. Worship began with personal prayers and meditation upon God's word, along with an interior knowledge and experience of God's amazing forgiveness and grace. Only afterward were found the external expressions of corporate worship and service to God as evidence of a life transformed, inside to outside.

The dichotomy between Catholic and Protestant spirituality in many ways continues even to this day. When the Anglican Church came into being, it was able to draw from each spiritual gene pool, to produce a kind of hybrid vigor. In much of the Anglican expression that follows, this external/internal tension between these spiritualities becomes part of a balanced whole.

In all fairness, both approaches to spirituality were contained within the Roman Catholic Church. Although both were nurtured down through time, the Protestant impulse generally found less favor with those in higher authority, as it was seen as a threat to the status quo. Following the Protestant Reformation there came a Catholic Counter-Reformation, which did indeed address many of the issues which fueled the Protestant fires. But, in the sixteenth century these two visions of being Christian came to a flashpoint over the sale of indulgences by the pope in Rome. Luther lit the fire of protest, and the rest, as they say, is history.

The ensuing conflict engulfed all of Western Europe, with political, social, and ecclesiastic upheaval and realignment. At the time, reformation meant bloodshed, as church and government, armies and populace fought out the passions of their beliefs. In time this fervor spread to England, and the Anglican Reformation was under way. Using the occasion of Henry the

VIII's marriage predicament, Thomas Cranmer[1] and the English reformers effected a split with Rome and brought about the establishment of the Anglican Church.

Cranmer was influenced by the continental reformers, and especially the Lutheran expression, which had been embraced by his wife. He longed to see a revitalized Christian faith in England, and a restoration of worship throughout the churches of the land. Cranmer's genius lay in his crafting of the Anglican Book of Common Prayer, as a means to bring order and conformity to every church in England. In this manner he reunified the community of faithful on a national scale, for all were to be engaged in same services of prayer on Sundays and throughout the week. In addition, Cranmer instituted the placing and reading of the Holy Scriptures in English in every parish, so that all could hear the word of God in their own language.

Henry VIII, who is commonly known as the founder of the Church of England, was unable to move forward with his own selfish desires for divorce and remarriage, because, as a Roman Catholic, he was subject to the authority of the pope. However, as the Reformation proceeded new jurisdictions were being formed based along ethnic and geographical lines, such as the Lutherans in Germany and the Reformed in Geneva. The monarchs, or rulers, of these jurisdictions were deemed to be the heads of the churches in their respective areas.

Cranmer and the other reformers approached Henry with a history lesson: before the Roman Catholic Church came to England and was established under the pope, there was already a Christian church present—the church of St. Patrick. Celtic Christianity had flourished first in Ireland and then throughout most of England from 432 to 597, until Rome sent St. Augustine to establish a Roman Catholic Church at Canterbury. As the Celtic Church and the Roman Church collided, the question needed to be addressed, "Which expression would be valid?" In 664 at the Synod of Whitby, King Oswy ruled in favor of Rome, and the Celtic Church faded from the scene. Therefore, Cranmer argued that as king, Henry VIII was actually the head of the church in England that existed before Rome ever arrived, and as such could reverse the earlier ruling and grant himself a divorce. Henry got what he wanted, a new marriage and chance for a male heir, but Cranmer and the others who desired reformation in England also achieved their goals, and the Anglican Church came into being.

1. See appendix 2, "Anglican-Ism Terms and Characters."

However, the conflict between Protestant and Catholic spiritualities, along with the resulting bloodshed, continued unabated until the populace was weary of religious strife. Finally, under the rule of Queen Elizabeth came the Anglican solution: the Via Media.

The Via Media

After years of bloody conflict between Catholic and Protestant forces in England, Elizabeth came to the throne. In a brilliant stroke of leadership, she gathered and reunified the English people around a new vision for the church and for the nation. Rather than being strictly Catholic or strictly Protestant, England would choose to compromise between them both: the Via Media, which literally means "middle way." Thus, the first Anglican Reformation was stabilized by maintaining that the church would retain the Catholic forms of worship—orders, liturgy and sacraments, symbols and vestments—while embracing the Protestant reforms of doctrine—sola scriptura, sola fide, sola gratia. The aptly named "Elizabethan Settlement" produced a beautifully harmonized English church, with a unity based in common prayer. Thereby, Anglicans maintained continuity with the Catholic tradition of the church, and embraced the Protestant return to the roots of Christianity and the authority of Holy Scripture. There remained, however, many who were deeply committed to one side or the other.

It should be added in fairness to the historical record that Elizabeth herself was not so deeply committed to the vision of a church balanced between Catholic and Protestant ideals. As sovereign of the Church of England, she was decidedly more Protestant in her views, especially since being so afforded her greater autonomy to rule according to her own will. The Via Media was a decidedly political solution for her as well as a theological one. Regardless of her intent, a de facto balance resulted from the continuation of sacramental, Catholic worship by the masses and the influx of Protestant ideals championed by the elite.

Catholic------------Church of England------------Protestant
(Via Media)

More than just a historical event, or a one-time decision, the Via Media, in and of itself, became a kind of doctrine to the Anglican Church. This principle of the middle way, and the willingness to allow for a central spectrum of beliefs and understanding, was a means by which ecclesiastical and doctrinal conflicts could be minimized and church unity strengthened. After the bloodshed of the Reformation period, Anglicans welcomed an approach to church life that allowed room for disagreement on the mysteries of the sacraments, while emphasizing the life of the community joined together in common prayer. Indeed, the Book of Common Prayer with its recollection of the Catholic Mass, Protestant emphasis on Scripture, and unifying quality of ecclesial practice may well be considered the icon of the Via Media down through history unto the present time. *Lex Orandi, Lex Credendi:* the law of praying is the law of believing; the law of believing is the law of living; a beautifully spiritual ideal that unites men and women of faith in a community of prayer, while giving grace for various doctrinal nuances.

The Via Media makes room for differences, gives place for discussion, and allows for agreement to disagree if needed without the breaking of fellowship. This principle works fine when the church and the surrounding culture are immersed in the Christian worldview, when the two visions at either end of the spectrum are Catholic Christian and Protestant Christian. However, as we shall see, such an approach leaves the Anglican-Ism vulnerable to radical change from an influx of non-Christian beliefs, especially when the principle of the middle way is applied to situations which include theologies and practices that are in conflict with those which are distinctly Christian.

In practice, the Via Media provided a stable vessel which sailed down through history and around the world, tacking sometimes port, to the Catholic side, sometimes starboard, to the Protestant side, while generally avoiding shipwreck on the reefs beyond the fringe. That is until the present day. This resiliency was due in no small part to the careful work in the beginning when the ship was built. As we continue, let us consider the work of the master craftsmen who laid the keel and set the sails.

The Early Apologists

The Anglican Church faced early challenges to its legitimacy, as well as the need for theological clarity in explaining this new expression of Christian faith and practice. The question still remained as to how to establish the legitimacy of the Church of England that would counter the claims of heresy, railed against it by Rome. These challenges and needs were addressed by two early apologists: John Jewel and Richard Hooker. Both sought to set the Anglican Church on a sure and certain course to navigate by.

John Jewel

In 1562, John Jewel's *Apology for the Church of England* was published, solidifying Queen Elizabeth's Protestant inclinations. Previously, Elizabeth had played her intentions close to the vest. Many of the populace hoped for, and saw signs, that she may return the English church to full communion with Rome. However, Protestant ideals and national pride had taken root in the English people, as well as their queen, and the schism with Rome was not to be rectified. Jewel's *Apology* takes up the task of legitimizing the Church of England from both a theological and ecclesiological standpoint. In doing so he supersedes and condemns the Church of Rome as apostate, and instead grounds the Church of England on the apostles, the primitive church, and the early fathers. What follows then is a summary of the main points of his argument.

Jewel's opening salvos in section one of the *Apology* refutes the charge of heresy. He portrays the Church of England as the faithful servant of God's truth, whom as a result is persecuted. Thus, he aligns the Church of England with Christ, Paul, and Stephen in the New Testament, and Isaiah, Jeremiah, and Daniel in the Old Testament. As they were persecuted, so also those who profess the gospel in England are also being persecuted. Having established solidarity with the prophets, apostles, and martyrs of Scripture, as well as Jesus Christ, Jewel further refutes the charges of heresy by insisting on a return to the doctrine of the fathers and primitive church. Finally, he asserts Holy Scripture as the final judge and arbiter of heresy, wresting away authority from the pope in matters of doctrine.

Jewel maintains the standard of Scripture was used by the "Holy Fathers," and that any judgment of heresy brought against the Church of England must be demonstrated thereof. He challenges and taunts the Catholics in a series of rhetorical questions accusing them of maintaining their own "dreams, cold inventions, and traditions" which have "corrupted the ordinances of Christ." Thus, he artfully turns the accusation of heresy back on the Catholics, while portraying the Church of England in the company of the faithful early church.

Having exonerated the Church of England from the accusation of heresy due to schism, Jewel continues with a clear articulation of the essence of what is believed. He provides a doctrinal dissertation that represents the foundation of Anglican Christianity. This portion of his *Apology* demonstrates the decidedly Protestant nature of the Church of England, in opposition to the strictly Catholic point of view. Continuing the theme of grounding the church in the apostolic fathers, Jewel begins with an affirmation of the Trinity that closely reflects the Nicene Creed. He affirms the offices of bishop, priest and deacon, and then argues against the supremacy of the bishop of Rome.

Thus, Jewel nullifies the preeminence of the pope, while retaining the conciliar bishopric of the early church. A move that is distinctly different from other reformers. The Protestant nature of Jewel's argument is further elucidated by several doctrinal positions. Marriage is sanctioned as holy for all persons, including priests. Two sacraments are affirmed: Baptism and Eucharist. Communion is to be given in both kinds. Both the bread and the wine are to be administered to the people. Also the doctrine of transubstantiation is expressly denied. Roman theology continued to hold that the bread and wine literally became the flesh and blood of Christ through a change in their substance.

Justification by faith, services said in English, and Christ as the only mediator complete Jewel's creed of Christian belief and closely aligned the Church of England with the continental reformers. In the heart of his *Apology*, Jewel lambastes the pope and Rome on the right, and severs all connection with fringe groups on the left. He compares the radical reformers—i.e., the Anabaptists—to previous heretical groups such as the Arians, Marcionites, etc. On the other hand the pope and his legates, along with the immoral practices and schemes for money, are all the subject of biting invective.

Throughout the remainder of his *Apology*, Jewel continues the themes of the apostasy and corruption of Rome, the solidarity of the Church of England with the primitive church, the authority of Scripture, and the equivalence of all bishops. He also adds a political justification by affirming the authority of the king in governing the church, granting examples from Scripture and history. The authority of the king is portrayed as God given, and above that of the pope. Even Henry VIII is vindicated. It must be noted that in this time there was no separation between church and state.

In reflection, Jewel's *Apology for the Church of England* is very thorough and convincing. He idealizes the English church as the pure, authentic expression of Christianity, artfully weaving connections with the apostles, the fathers, and the primitive church. The Church of England is true Christianity which has shaken itself free from the corruption of Rome. He turns the charge of heresy back on the accusers, redefines authority to exclude preeminence by the pope, and exalts the power and position of the

Monarch. Throughout, he establishes a decidedly Protestant charter for the Church of England, and vindicates Queen Elizabeth as its head.

Richard Hooker

Whereas Jewel sought to vindicate the Church of England from the charges of heresy, and to establish it as a faithful continuation of the early church, Richard Hooker took a step further in defining Anglican theological belief. Hooker is an important father of the Anglican-Ism, one who is often quoted in support of the various theological positions today. Yet, one that is also often misunderstood when attempting to apply his thought to our current historical context. In particular, his promotion of three authoritative sources for Christian belief and practice: Scripture, tradition, and reason. Over time Hooker's approach has become known as the "three-legged stool."

Richard Hooker lived at the time of the Reformation, and was thoroughly immersed in the late medieval worldview. In his time the world was understood in a hierarchical fashion. God was a God of order, who fashioned creation and society in such a manner that it displayed that order. Each person had their place in society, and the grace of God trickled down through his anointed monarchs and the church unto the rest of the people.

Hooker's theology describes this order in terms of law: celestial law governs the angelic beings in the cosmic hierarchy that is above us; the law of nature concerns our physical universe and its underlying forces; the law of reason comes out of the moral principles formed out of human conscience that is separate from theological knowledge; and divine law embraces godly principles through infused revelation, the Bible, and the way of salvation through faith in Jesus Christ.

In Hooker's view of reality, the fallible and contradictory nature of reason is redeemed through the use of divine law, or Scripture, bringing correction when necessary. The senses, imagination, common sense, and the will all combine together to inform a person. Reason is the highest faculty which orders the rest. Yet, due to the fall these faculties no longer function according to their original design. They are scrambled, with reason vying for control over other baser instincts. Salvation results in a right ordering by the Holy Spirit, a reorientation to right the system and to divine law.

Human reason is thereby restored to its rightful place in the hierarchy of the universe. In keeping with the standards of the Reformation, that hierarchy includes the primacy of Scripture and deference to the monarch, as head of the church. The queen was God's anointed, who ruled in matters of tradition, especially where Scripture is silent.

Thus, we find in Hooker a holistic system of authority, which resonates from the top down, beginning with God and flowing through his appointed channels and social institutions. Individual identity and authority was drawn from a person's place in the whole. Reason has its place within the hierarchy, rather than standing apart from it in judgment. Authority resides in God and is expressed by his law, instead of the individual who asserts authority over the universe.

Unfortunately, the metaphor of the "three-legged stool" purported to come from Hooker as a model of authority, is currently entrenched in minds of many, if not most Anglicans. This popular sentiment seeks to affirm and balance Scripture, tradition and reason as the three sources from which authority is derived. Richard Hooker, the "Father of Anglicanism," is often attributed with devising this three-legged model, but upon closer historical analysis the evidence weighs heavily against such a conclusion. This concept came into being through a historical context and worldview that is radically different from that of Richard Hooker. The model itself is highly problematic, and fraught with presuppositions that are antithetical to Hooker's thought.

The concept of the three-legged stool as a model for authority in the Anglican Church developed as a consequence of three primary strands of ecclesial expression gaining prominence in the time period after the Enlightenment: the evangelicals, the Anglo-Catholics and the liberals. These three parties coexisting in one church allowed a superficial illusion to emerge that espoused three different sources of truth as their basis, namely Scripture, tradition and reason. This led to the image of the three legs of a stool, each source being equal to the other. The evangelicals favored Scripture, the Anglo-Catholics looked to tradition, and the liberals espoused reason as primacy.

The three parties listed above do indeed place particular emphasis on each of their respective "legs." Yet, the fusion of Scripture, tradition and reason that occurred post Hooker embodied Enlightenment presuppositions that were radically different. Human reason was exalted to the position of final arbiter of truth in the modern era. And though the three-legged stool is purported to be a metaphor for authority in the Anglican Church, the modern or Enlightenment worldview establishes the individual as the objective autonomous decision maker. Thus, each person is portrayed as having authority to objectively decide how to use the sources of Scripture, tradition, and reason. Since, reason is in reality the primary faculty of the autonomous individual, in effect, this is where authority resides. Scripture and tradition may only have influence according to the measure afforded to them by what the individual deems reasonable.

So then, the metaphor of the three-legged stool as representative of authority in the Anglican Church is a modern idea, grounded in the Enlightenment presuppositions of the autonomy of the individual and the ascendancy of reason. Reason itself being held as purely objective and virtually infallible. But this does not compare with Hooker's views on reason and authority, as well as his understanding of Scripture and tradition. Hooker wrote extensively about human reason, but it is clear that he was referring to something completely different.[2]

Hooker's understanding of the nature of reason was that it was fallible requiring divine law, or Scripture, to bring correction. This contrasts radically with the autonomous reason of modernity which denies any exterior authority and uses tangible facts to draw objective conclusions. In Hooker's epistemology reason is one of several faculties which are designed to interface with the created order as a God-given receptor/processor that enables humans to understand divine laws and the world around us.

Scripture, tradition, and reason are not three wells which individual Anglicans draw from at will to support their own autonomous authority. They are not some mythological stool upon which Anglicanism sits. Hooker in particular did not believe this. The interface of Scripture, tradition and reason is much more complicated. The God given faculty of reason enables us to make sense out of the creation around us, and to partake of divine revelation via the Scripture. The Scripture informs tradition, the ongoing life of the community of believers, and the community interprets Scripture in the present. Ultimately authority resides in God himself. His authority is manifested by means of the Holy Spirit through the Scripture and the community. Reason may be thought of as that combination of faculties which enable us to encounter and know God, but never as an independent judge over the truth of his revelation.

---

2. See Fairfield, *Lecture on Richard Hooker*.

Anglican Comprehensiveness

Jewel and Hooker maintained and expanded the Anglican-Ism, widening the walls to allow for Catholic form and offices, while maintaining Protestant ideals of Scripture and faith. In the process, the way was made to incorporate the prevailing understanding of reason and authority, thus strengthening and expanding the Via Media even further. In Hooker we see the beginning of the interaction of the church with the ideals of the surrounding culture. The Enlightenment period upheld reason as the highest value, and Hooker brought reason into the matrix of the middle way, in order to balance it with Scripture and tradition. Thus, we see an acknowledgement of the values of modernity, which then becomes an ongoing practice as history unfolds—the importation of values and ideas from the surrounding culture into the matrix of the Via Media.

The stage was set, the foundation laid, comprehensiveness was now in the DNA of Anglicanism. A principle was established that allowed for a spectrum of belief. Catholic and Protestant poles had been established and affirmed, and now the challenge to find the balance was to begin. As we move down through the history that follows, the pendulum begins to swing back and forth from one side to the other, with each swing bringing more into the mix. Let us consider two important movements which continue to exert influence to this day: the Evangelical Revival and the Oxford Movement.

In mode of operation the Via Media spread out its branches over both the Catholic and Protestant ideals, seeking to gather as much as possible into the center. This resulted in a comprehensiveness that made room for subtle differences of belief, along with more contradictory assertions of faith. Anglican comprehensiveness reflects that proper polite, and somewhat stoic, model of English sensibility. No one wanted to return to the religious conflicts of the past, so, for heaven's sake, let's agree to disagree and maintain unity through common worship with the Book of Common Prayer.

The principle of this comprehensive unity has continued even to this day. At times, it has allowed for marvelous interactions and synthesis of Christian thought. Especially since those with new understandings were not burned alive as heretics. However, at other times Anglican comprehensiveness alone was insufficient to contain, or retain, movements that pulled out in new directions—movements such as the Evangelical Revival, led by the Wesleys and George Whitefield. Evangelicals today may be surprised to learn they started out as Anglicans.

Evangelical Revival

The ideal of comprehensiveness embraced by Anglicans was in practice difficult to keep in balance. The Catholic and Protestant components did not always stay grafted together, but sought to pull back to their respective roots. This is what began to occur in the eighteenth century in a movement that has become well known as the Evangelical Revival. The evangelical principles remain as an integral part of the Anglican Church unto this day, and so it is important for our purposes to understand how this expression formed, and the components which maintain its vibrancy.

Throughout the history of Christianity there has run concurrent with the institutional expression of the church an impulse which focuses on personal devotion and deep individual spirituality. Perhaps within our being there also resides this distinction between the mind, the seat of rationality, and the heart, the vessel of passion. The institutional church, with its structures and doctrines, orders the faith after the rational faculty of the mind. While much of this process may be reflected on with a positive light, faith may become a dry rehearsal of objective propositions without the balance of a passionate spirituality. Such is the case with the evangelical revival that began in the 1600s in Germany and spread to England and America. The impulse of personal and devotional spirituality took root in German Pietism, branched out by means of the Wesleyan movement in England, and flowered in the Great Awakening of colonial America. By tracing the development of this evangelical offshoot we are able to examine the fruit of the movement and the similarities and differences of each phase of its growth.

John Wesley, an Anglican, was a paradigmatic figure whose encounter with the evangelical impulse radically altered the course of his own life, and the history of Christianity in England. As a young missionary on route to Georgia, Wesley was impressed by the faith of a group of German Pietists, and the peace they maintained in the midst of a life threatening storm in the North Atlantic. Wesley, who had fervently disciplined his life in the religious expression of the time, found himself fearful and lacking in the confidence of these early evangelicals. Like Luther before him, Wesley had given religion his best, yet come up short. Later, at a Pietist meeting back in England, Wesley had a conversion experience in which God's love and

Anglican-Ism

grace were realized when his "heart was strangely warmed" upon hearing a reading from Romans.

> In the evening I went very unwillingly to a society in Aldersgate Street, where one was reading Luther's preface to the Epistle to the Romans. About a quarter before nine, while he was describing the change which God works in the heart through faith in Christ, I felt my heart strangely warmed. I felt I did trust in Christ, Christ alone, for salvation; and an assurance was given me that He had taken away my sins, even mine, and saved me from the law of sin and death.[3]

Wesley was primed to develop the Evangelical revival in its English phase. Like the Pietist before him, he held Scriptures in high esteem, both in preaching and teaching. The evangelical emphasis on personal experience vs. doctrinal correctness was born out in his own conversion. The zeal to proclaim the gospel welled up within Wesley—the gospel of personal relationship with a personal God. He built upon German Pietism by modifying missionary zeal to include social reform, especially regarding alcoholism and slavery, and stressed the need for a conversion experience as distinct in validating faith, and as an assurance of salvation.

Wesley went out preaching in the open markets and fields to crowds of common people who thronged to hear him. The birth of revivalism in England was occasioned by conversion experiences, repentance and deliverance from alcohol—the demon gin. Wherever Wesley preached he organized and left behind fellowship groups designed to focus on Bible study and discipleship. The rigorous structure of these groups was attributed to his "methods" for spiritual growth. Hence, the "Methodists" became the evangelical movement in England.

Meanwhile in America some years prior, another seedling of revival had sprung up in New England through the preaching of Jonathan Edwards. Edwards, a Calvinist and Puritan who was also influenced by the Pietists, suddenly experienced an intense spiritual excitement among his congregation in response to his preaching. This enthusiasm quickly spread to other congregations throughout New England. Itinerant preachers such as Cotton Mather and William Tennent kept the revival fires burning from town to town. Edwards chronicled three hundred conversions in the first year in his publication, *Christian History*, which was devoted to journaling the revivals.

3. Wesley, "I Felt My Heart."

Anglican Manifesto

The English evangelical impulse intersected with America through the person of George Whitefield. Whitefield was a close friend of John Wesley, and traveled to America to preach in 1740. A masterful orator who trained for the stage before giving his life to preach, Whitefield so captivated his American crowds that it was reported he could bring tears to the eye simply by saying the word Mesopotamia. He toured up and down the eastern seaboard unifying the local revivals into the Great Awakening. Like the German and English counterparts the revival of the Great Awakening stressed the need for conversion and personal experience with God.

The three manifestations of the Evangelical Revival—German Pietism, the Wesleyan movement in England, and the Great Awakening in America—expressed many common elements. All developed as a response to a dry cognitive propositionalist form of Christianity that emphasized rational forms of worship and the correctness of right belief over the living out of a holy life. They emphasized the priesthood of all believers grounding religion in the experience of a personal relationship with a personal God. Scripture was given a high status as God's revelation so that preaching, teaching and Bible study gained preeminence as an expression of discipleship. The evangelical ferment included prayer and activism both on the mission field and in society at large—a desire to spread the Word of God to change lives and society. To sum up, Evangelicals embodied biblicism, activism in mission and social concern, individual spiritual devotion and prayer, and the living out of ones faith as opposed to mere intellectual assent.

The Evangelical Revival that came as a reformation to the Reformation has left its legacy on the history of Christianity. Whenever Christian faith becomes dry or unfruitful through mere intellectual reasoning or cultural accommodation, there has been a fresh move within the church toward a more personal, living spirituality. This Evangelical impulse has threaded its way down through history, finding expression in such forms as the Hussites or the Franciscans, and in individuals like Bernard of Clairvox, Peter Abelard, or Soren Kirkegaard. The danger with this kind of spirituality, that grounds itself in the intuitive, emotional, existential faculties of our being, is that it may begin to focus too much on the experience of the individual—thus being reduced to an enthusiasm that in and of itself becomes a detriment to community. Nevertheless, without the vibrancy of devotion, personal relationship with God, and the experience of his love, faith becomes just one more proposition that, even if true, barely intersects with the rest of our lives. The Evangelical Revival will continue to represent a vibrant expression of Christian life and ministry that we may draw upon to strengthen our own discipleship and spiritual growth.

In our discussion on the continuing development of the Anglican-Ism, it is important to understand how the Evangelical Revival both refined and redefined the Protestant side of the equation. Protestant ideals from the Reformation were clarified by the evangelicals, who effectively claimed ownership of the Protestant pole within the Anglican Church. Thus, we can consider the two poles at either end of the spectrum Catholic and evangelical Protestant, that is until the Protestant side further divides. Anglican evangelicals were Christocentric, holding Christ and the cross at the center of all theology. They espoused: biblicism, a high view of the authority of Scripture; activism, an intense engagement with the social issues of the day; and the need for a conversion experience, which resulted in personal faith and piety with Jesus.

This distillation of Protestant principles out of the Catholic/Protestant elixir, set the stage for further distillation to come, as liberal and charismatic movements pull out to create two additional poles, or expressions within the Anglican stream. As we shall see further on, this resulted in four poles within Anglicanism, a quad that forms a kind of theological grid contained in the vessel of the Via Media. Following the Protestant fervor of the Evangelical Revival, which had begun with the Anglicans but soon jumped out of the Church of England to form new denominations in America, the pendulum swung back toward the Catholic side with the Oxford Movement.

The Oxford Movement

The Oxford Movement, which emphasized apostolic succession, the authority of tradition, and communion as the center of Christian worship, began in earnest with the preaching of John Keble's sermon on July 14, 1833. The issue at hand was a reform of the Church of Ireland, which was directed by laws passed in Parliament. Keble, professor of poetry at Oxford, vehemently attacked the principle of secular authority being exercised over the church. The sermon catalyzed a group of fellows which included Richard Froude, Edward Pusey, and John Henry Newman. Together they initiated an aggressive movement of reform in the Church of England, writing a series of tracts against nominalism and abuse, and exhorting greater piety. The times were ripe for such a reform movement to flourish. The Oxford

Movement rose to prominence by reviving the old high church tradition, and infusing it with new vitality by adding elements from the Evangelical Movement and Romanticism.

The Oxford fellows embraced a high view of the Church of England which had been advocated by William Laud and the Arminians. They looked to the primitive apostolic church as the ideal, and sought strict obedience to church tradition. Indeed, the tradition of the church was affirmed as an equal authority with Scripture, the two strands running parallel with one another down through history. Thus, the historic episcopate retained authority in all matters of church polity, and should in no way be superseded by the secular authority of Parliament.

The earlier high church tradition had understood the Church of England as the genuine expression of catholicity, supplanting Rome as the legitimate progeny of the primitive church. The Roman Catholic Church had strayed and allowed a laxity in worship, which required the rigorous corrective of the Reformation. The Church of England was also in danger of slipping away from an authentic and vibrant practice of the faith, and therefore needed a high, or stiff, disposition.[4]

To be a high churchman was to maintain unfailing commitment to the bishops and traditions of the church, and guard them against dissent and radicalism.

Along with the affirmation of Apostolic Succession, the Oxford Movement drew upon several other elements in the legacy of the high stream of Anglicanism. They held the church fathers in high regard, looking to them for theological inspiration over the continental reformers. Liturgical worship in the "beauty of holiness" was preferred over the austerity of the Puritans. Also, the sacrament of Holy Communion maintained preeminence, with tracts encouraging more frequent celebration.

The pendulum had swung back to the Catholic side of the Via Media, in celebration of the Catholic forms of worship. Of course, these high church proclivities opened the Oxford Movement to Puritan criticism, and charges of popery, as it had done to their predecessors. While the Oxford Movement embraced the high expression of church life in many ways it differed subtly by drawing in elements and attitudes found in other quarters. Along with structured, "high," community life, the Oxford fellows desired an experience of God and personal piety that was reflective of the Evangelicals. Theirs was a worship of the heart not just the head.

---

4. Chadwick, *Mind of the Oxford Movement*, 14.

The final major influence upon the Oxford Movement is found in the very socio-historical context in which it was birthed. The early nineteenth century witnessed a large scale reaction to enlightenment rationality, commonly known as Romanticism. The romantic impulse is evidenced in the Oxford Movement through their intuitive approach to encounter with God by means of sacrament and worship. The Oxford fellows delighted in poetry and aesthetic beauty in the worship of God, and stepped away from rational argumentation as a means of proving the truth of the gospel.

The Oxford Movement drew upon elements of Romanticism, high church tradition, and evangelical belief to formulate a vision of an authoritative church community. This community was to be the Church of England. Under the leadership of John Henry Newman and the acuity of his contemporaries, the movement became a force for renewal in the eighteen-thirties and forties. Their ideas were disseminated through inexpensive tracts, earning them the name Tractorians. Eventually, Newman himself "swam the Tiber" and converted to Roman Catholicism, and the Movement splintered amid growing resistance from without and differing opinions from within. Yet, the Oxford Movement retained a lasting impact on Anglicanism, affirming Episcopal polity, encouraging worship in the beauty of holiness, and reemphasizing Holy Communion as the center of Christian worship.

The acceptance and incorporation of the expressions embodied by the Oxford Movement and Evangelical Revival, further expanded and strengthened the principle of Anglican comprehensiveness. As a result, the way was made for yet new arrivals of thought and practice to also come in to the Anglican fold, as they emerged from their current historical paradigms.

In response to the attacks of higher criticism in the modern period, a liberal Protestant expression emerged. Liberal Protestantism split out from the evangelicals taking with them the focus on social activism as the heart of the gospel. The emphasis on conversion experience became simply spiritual experience, and biblicism was set aside in the light of modern reason. So, Anglicanism now had three poles of Christian expression within: catholic, evangelical, and liberal.

As history flows a bit further into the twentieth century, the charismatic revivals began to take place. Taking spiritual experience in a different direction, the main emphasis was now on the power and gifts of the Holy Spirit within the church in our time. At first this movement was contained within the existing vessels of church expression, but soon moved out to become a pole in and of itself. Thus, as we come down through time to the present we find Catholic and Protestant further developed into catholic, evangelical, liberal, and charismatic. All accepted within the Anglican fold, due to the principle of comprehensiveness which we found from the beginning.

The danger with this quiet comprehensive approach to Christian faith and practice is that eventually it can simply become an excuse to allow anyone to believe anything that seems proper to themselves. Like a man who eats whatever he likes, whenever he wants, eventually he will end up unable to move. Comprehensiveness leads to inertia. In order to get back to life he must have some discipline and exercise. In like manner in order to be healthy and energetic, Anglican comprehensiveness must engage in the more difficult task of going on a diet from time to time.

Autonomous Fellowship and the Chicago-Lambeth Quadrilateral

The Anglican Church grew and the Anglican-Ism expanded exponentially along with the British Empire. Colonialism meant that Anglican churches were planted in countries around the world. Province by province the Church of England was transformed into a church of the world—the Anglican Communion. Provinces were set up that essentially mirrored the polity of the original, with bishops and archbishops in authority. What emerged from this process is another guiding principle of Anglican-Ism, that being one of autonomous fellowship.

Each province of the Anglican Church was deemed to be autonomous. That is to say that there was no central adjudicating authority, such as the Roman Catholic pope, or even perhaps a metropolitan of the Orthodox Church. While individual differences did develop within the various polities of the provinces, all adhered to the autonomous rule of the bishops, who were duly consecrated in turn from those who preceded them. This allowed for the ability to flex and adjust to local context. It has been said that this principle of autonomy was the genius of the Anglican-Ism. More recently it has been said the same lack of a central authority has proved to be the Anglican-Ism's Achilles' heel.

Autonomous fellowship developed as a desire for the sharing of church life across the nations in a way that was non-coercive, and in a manner that did not give power to the powerful. That is to say, this allowed for the Anglican churches that were planted during colonialism, to become un-colonial by being able to provide oversight for themselves.

The principle of autonomy did not necessarily promote the independence of each province to do as they pleased; instead, it affirmed the interdependence of each province, as equals with one another. Once again, we must remember that, by and large, there was widespread agreement of Christian belief and practice. The Book of Common Prayer, the Via Media, and in general a Christian worldview were prevalent throughout the eighteenth and nineteenth centuries, until Christendom began grappling with the paradigm shift of modernity. Nevertheless, as we approach the twentieth century, questions begin to be raised: What is Anglican-Ism? How will we define who or what we are? What is the nature of the relationship between professing Anglican churches? Novel concepts it would seem, because for the most part the whole ethos, the Anglican-Ism, was just taken for granted.

In order to answer the questions of relationship, communion, and commonality, Anglican bishops from around the world came together in council and discussion, first in Chicago in 1886, then two years later at Lambeth, England, in 1888. The result was the production of the four basic tenets that defined the Anglican Communion. The Chicago-Lambeth Quadrilateral declares this is what defines us as Anglicans, that to which all agree upon and binds our common life together:

1. The Holy Scriptures of the Old and New Testament as the revealed Word of God.
2. The Nicene Creed as the sufficient statement of the Christian Faith.
3. The two Sacraments—Baptism and the Supper of the Lord—ministered with the unfailing use of Christ's words of institution and of the elements ordained by Him.
4. The Historic Episcopate, locally adapted in the methods of its administration to the varying needs of the nations and peoples called of God into the unity of His Church.[5]

Thus, autonomous fellowship remained as the order of the day, along with a fresh articulation of the four cornerstones upon which rested the Anglican Cathedral. This fourfold description of Anglican belief and practice remains definitive unto this day, and was sufficient to handle the challenges

---

5. See appendix 1, *Chicago-Lambeth Quadrilateral*.

of the modern era. The problem being that, now, we are no longer living in the modern era, as we shall discuss in the next chapter on paradigms.

The Big Tent

The twentieth century witnessed the expansion of the theological/ecclesial spectrum within the Anglican-Ism in several significant ways. As mentioned previously, the polarity between Catholic and Protestant, morphed into a grid with four distinct expressions: catholic, evangelical, charismatic, and liberal. Each of these had their own particular theological emphasis, spirituality, and agenda. Thus, the two poles of the Anglican-Ism became four, all set within the borders of the Anglican Communion. Yet, all continued to touch upon the broader developing historical streams of Christianity in general. The Anglican Church became a big tent, where it would seem everyone was welcome. A place where differences were set aside and all could be together regardless of particular theologies and practices.

Fast forwarding to the present, then, what we find in operation as a principle of common life is the concept of the big tent. All are welcome to come in, the doors open outward, and inward, in all directions. Inside the big tent there is a lot of activity. We find not just the typical three ring circus, but four: four centers of spirituality; four centers of theology; four grandstands gathering four communities around centers of activity and purpose. The big tent represents the culmination of the comprehensiveness inherent in the Church of England from the beginning. As noted earlier, this was the genius of the Anglican-Ism, and now, this has also become its downfall.

Within the tent, we find four Baptismal fonts filled from the historic streams of Christian expression, but with little connection or accountability between them. Each is steadily baptizing converts into their own respective systems of belief. Within the tent, we find all the excitement, the energy, the pageantry of a four ring circus, but no ringmaster to coordinate, or oversee the results. The tent itself is held up by the four poles of the Lambeth Quadrilateral, but there are no side panels—no boundaries to the outside world. Thus, the big tent is vulnerable to collapse when the winds blow.

Conclusion

There definitely *is* an Anglican stream of Christianity flowing from the Reformation of the sixteenth century, a mixture of tributaries that flow from the headwaters of Catholic and Protestant ecclesiology. Along the way, other tributaries have joined in; evangelical, charismatic, and liberal currents have become well established. And so, the Anglican Church is now multifaceted, with a broad spectrum of theological beliefs and practices. For better or worse, comprehensiveness and the dictum to find the middle way comprise major components of the Anglican expression of Christianity as it flows forward in history.

The principle of openness among the churches of the communion and to the world, is expressed through a sense of autonomy and willingness to adapt to the surrounding cultural context. The benefit of openness has allowed the Anglican-Ism to spread worldwide, bringing the church to a multitude of different languages and peoples. Yet, now this same openness leaves a vulnerability to the reverse as well. Instead of the gospel flowing out to the surrounding culture, the ideologies of the surrounding culture have flowed backwards into the church. Indeed, I would argue that the Anglican Church has no inherent boundaries within itself. Rather, in openness it has allowed the surrounding culture to set the boundaries for it. Hence, when a major paradigm shift occurs, the boundaries are subject to readjustment, or in being discarded altogether.

Anglican Manifesto

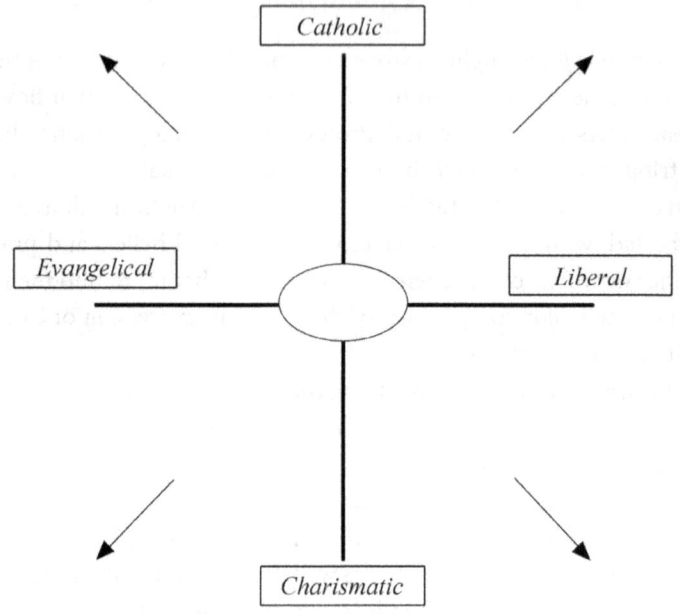

The four poles of Christian expression incorporated into the Anglican-Ism
Arrows depict the intentional movement or promotion to the surrounding world
Note: There are no boundaries to prevent the reversal of the arrows
Thereby allowing the world to flow into the church

The graph above is representative of the Anglican Church today. The four poles of Christian expression are not only indicative of the Anglican-Ism, but are also true of the Christian church as a whole. Historically, the river of Christianity has split into a variety of streams and rivulets. The process began with the Great Schism of 1054, which divided Eastern Orthodox with Roman Catholic expressions. The Reformation separated the Protestant stream from within the Western tributary, forming Lutheran, Reformed, Anglican and Anabaptist variations. Subsequently, Protestants continued to split from one another, as evangelical, liberal, and charismatic expressions formed and went off on their own ways.

Practically speaking these four streams of Christianity, which were all present in the beginning, continue to incorporate the major portions of the worldwide church in our time. This is the community of the church, as practiced by the faithful, and as seen by the world. Indeed, each of the four streams has captured and contained within itself a portion of the gospel of Jesus Christ, vibrant elements which are part of the whole. Churches have then polarized around their own particular elements of the faith, most often to the exclusion of the others. What all need to realize is that each of the four make up a vital part of the whole. In fact, I will argue that they all need each other to stay in balance. Separated from one another in isolation each and every expression has more potential to go off track—to flow off on a tangent leaving genuine Christianity behind.

The Anglican Church, the church of the Via Media, not surprisingly finds itself flowing in the middle of the streambeds. All four of these major expressions have been accepted as valid within the Anglican-Ism. But, this is not to say they have been all brought together in a balanced whole. Usually individual churches within the Anglican stream embrace and polarize around one or the other of these poles just like the more broadly defined streams of the church as a whole. Nevertheless, the potential for wholeness does reside in the Anglican Church. It is here that all are included, all are able to inform one another, all correct one another, and all contribute to a sum which is greater than the individual parts.

Furthermore, as the church in the middle of it all, Anglicans are uniquely situated in Christendom to bring together the major streams flowing around them. They all share a connection of one expression or another that is already accepted in Anglican-Ism. Thus, we have a common starting point from which we can relate to one another. We have a mode of fellowship and understanding already in place. Being in the middle means Anglicans can talk to everyone.

Where would you locate your church on the graph? My goal in writing this manifesto is to bring us all to the center.

The Anglican-Ism is comprehensive, it is open, and it has vitality. It has from the beginning been a fervent mix of many of the vibrant expression of Christian faith, which are themselves often polarized and isolated within their own church contexts. Catholic, evangelical, charismatic, and liberal streams, when allowed to inform and balance one another, have great potential to enhance and create a wholeness in worship and community life that is much needed to engage the world in the emerging paradigm of the twenty-first century. On a personal note, this is why I became an Anglican to begin with.

In order to be effective, and, at the same time overcome the vulnerabilities which have led to the current crisis in the Anglican Communion, the Anglican-Ism which has brought us this far needs adjustment. Before moving to a discussion of the immediate problems and solutions, first let us consider the paradigm shifts through which the Anglican-Ism has already come, and the one which is now upon us, in the next chapter—"Paradigm to Paradigm."

Paradigm Shift:
A change in a fundamental model of events
—THOMAS KUHN

2

Paradigm to Paradigm

History flows down through time like a mighty river reaching for the sea—an Amazon of human ideas, events and understanding. At times, when the river is deep and wide, the surface like glass can barely be perceived as moving at all. The culture is content and in agreement with the prevalent values, religion, science and moral understanding of the day. These taken together comprise the reigning paradigm.

Yet, like a mighty river there are other occasions when the banks narrow and the water begins to swirl and boil. Rapids appear as the force of steeply dropping new terrain stirs the water from bottom to top. In these historical moments we observe a paradigm shift in which prevailing values and norms are critically reassessed and discarded if deemed no longer useful. The old paradigm is torn down and a new era emerges in the light of new discovery, as a result of changing social conditions, or due to frustration with the consequences of the old attitudes, values, or governance. The banks narrow. The rocks appear. The old paradigm is torn to pieces. The ideas of the old way which may still hold value and are deemed worthy may find a place in the new, but those which do not are discarded as time and history stabilize and the banks of the river widen once again.

The term paradigm comes from the philosophy of science and is defined as a "generally accepted model of how ideas relate to one another and form a conceptual framework, which scientific research is then carried out within." Paradigms exist within science, but they are not limited to science. We all have our own personal paradigm—our beliefs, values, activities and routines that enable us to function. Societies function through relationships made possible by mutual assent to the reigning paradigm, those beliefs that are commonly held and known to be right. Although we rarely give thought to its existence, paradigms provide the operating system that allows us to function and to interact with one another. Over time these modes of operation become entrenched in whole eras of history. That is until the next version comes along.

Socio-historical paradigms are just that, a particular ordering of social interactions and understanding within a historical time period. One that provides an operating system that allows the society to function. While this type of paradigm is definitely real, it is mostly invisible. It exists beneath the surface in the assumptions of what is true, and the presuppositions of what is real. It becomes self-perpetuating through a myriad of subtle communications, which we intuitively receive and incorporate into our lives. In this manner we just know what is and is not proper behavior without even consciously thinking about it.

The components of a historical paradigm are scientific, technological, religious, spiritual, and even emotional. Our values, beliefs, morals/ethics, and rituals are embedded in the paradigm that surrounds us. We believe the world is what it is because it feels right. All the complexities of human data and interaction feed into the formation of the reigning paradigm. This is mostly invisible, beneath the conscious awareness within social exchanges, but often readily seen in the artwork of an era, or now, especially in the films and TV ads that provide our reflection in the mirror.

Paradigms reign because they work, at least for a time and in the time of their historical era. The agreed-upon elements remain in place until they are cast down by new irrefutable insights, become irrelevant, or simply cease to function because the world has moved on. When the telephone was invented, the telegraph ceased to exist. When cell phones came to be land lines ceased. When they invent the microchip that inserts into the bone above your ear, cell phones will no longer be needed. Paradigm to paradigm. This simple illustration has been played out on a much larger scale throughout history. In ancient times Ptolemy demonstrated that the earth was the center of the universe. Everyone knew it was true. It felt right. It affected the way we understood our humanity. Then came the Renaissance and the Copernican revolution. The previous era in history was overturned, and the sun became the center of the universe. This change set off a chain reaction amongst the other elements throughout the reigning paradigm, testing and trying them for relevance in the new order. A paradigm shift was underway.

The process of shifting from paradigm to paradigm has been a common occurrence in Western history. A certain way of living and being a society gains ascendency and makes sense of the facts and values present in a particular time period. An operating system develops that functions and continues until it begins to decay. At times new facts emerge, which then unravel the system. Assumptions are proven to be false, or generally accepted principles no longer hold together. The shift begins to a new, revised set of criteria, often accompanied by a period of uncertainty and anxiety until things settle into place once again. A new paradigm emerges.

The new paradigm makes sense to the culture and to the time. Populace, governance, education, and religious institutions all readjust to keep step with the new paradigm. Most importantly, in the collective conscious, or perhaps subconscious, the basic assumptions and presuppositions of the new paradigm become the accepted norms for social interaction. Everyone knows, or comes to understand, and agrees that this is the right way to think and act. The lens of the new paradigm becomes the way in which the world around us is viewed and accepted by everyone. Well, almost everyone.

With every paradigm shift there are always those holdouts, those who remain stuck in the old way of thinking. But, as the river flows onward, time wears them down and pushes them aside into quiet eddies alongside that swirl. They become trapped in their own momentum. These eddies are often viewed as irrelevant and antiquated by the main stream, or at times even threatening or intolerable. They are the ones who simply don't get it and refuse to go along with the program.

Anglican Manifesto

All institutions of society must adjust to the new paradigms when they come. The church in particular often faces great challenges, especially when the dogma, worship, and morality promoted by the church are perceived as threats to the new order of the day. This is true when the church, or elements within the church, are viewed as irrelevant, or ineffective, and seen as part of the problems of the past rather than the solutions for the present. In these times the pressure mounts for them to be discarded. The adjustment between church, culture, and the new paradigm is further complicated by virtue of the fact that the church itself is also totally immersed in the surrounding culture, the people who make up the church also live, work, and participate daily in the world. Thus, the members of the church will also be influenced toward the position of the new paradigm, thinking along with the world that it is right and good and that it makes sense.

At times the church may find itself in active participation with the shift. Sometimes the changes made fit hand in hand with the traditional biblical viewpoint, as in the case of the abolishment of slavery during the paradigm shift of the Enlightenment. Sometimes the changes are more accommodating to the surrounding culture, as in the present day case of same sex marriage. Due to the conservative nature of the church throughout most of Western history we more often find ourselves on the defensive, at odds with society or at least with key principles of each succeeding paradigm shift. This, I believe, is one of the essential calls of the Christian church, to be a prophetic witness to all generations.

For our purposes it is important to note how much the church is a participant of the reigning paradigm in contrast with how much it stands apart, either in isolation or prophetic witness. Paradigm to paradigm, what are some of the key changes that have taken place in society, and how have they elicited change in turn from the church? The challenge to the church in general is to continue to faithfully preach the gospel, the faith once delivered to the saints, within the context of the historical paradigm in which we live. The holy mystery of the church, which is the body of Christ, is designed to present to every age the certainty of salvation through Jesus Christ, in a manner that is relevant, yet, at the same time uncompromising—a sacramental witness that speaks directly to the hearts, minds, and souls of the world around us.

The strength of the Anglican Church has been its flexibility in adapting to the paradigm shifts of Western civilization. The elements that constitute the Anglican-Ism form a broad spectrum of contact points between

Christian faith and the secular world, which when functioning properly allow the gospel to flow outward into society at large. The weakness of the Anglican Church is that when proper boundaries are not maintained the flow is reversed, and the secular world flows into the church. The Anglican-Ism then becomes an extension of the Human-Ism.

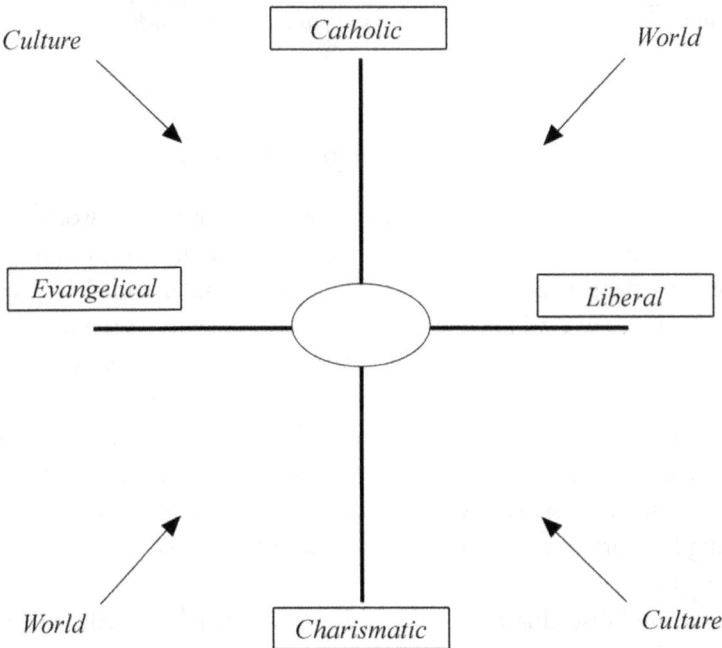

**The four poles of Christian expression incorporated into the Anglican-Ism
Arrows depict the intentional movement in from the surrounding world**

If we were to make an analysis of historical paradigm shifts all the way back to ancient times, we would observe an ever increasing closeness of cultures, economies, and religions, along with an ever decreasing constriction of time in between each shift. Because we are concerned with an Anglican perspective, we will engage the process from the time of the Reformation, and the paradigm in which the Church of England came into being. Let us take a brief survey through the major paradigm shifts, considering the social contexts, prevailing values, and some of the ways the Anglican Church adapted in each era.

Anglican Manifesto

Paradigm	Social Context	Values	Adaptation
Premodern	Western Christian	Tradition	Catholic
Modern	Enlightenment	Reason	Via Media
Postmodern	Pluralism	Experience	Spirituality
Oneworld*	Unified	Participation	Community

*So named by the author to describe the next paradigm shift which is already upon us

The Premodern Paradigm

In the premodern era, Christians espoused a sacramental worldview in which the spiritual realm infused the material realm with meaning, purpose, and danger. By means of ritual a person intertwined his/her life with the grace of God flowing through the sacraments. As the devil strove for dominion over the souls of men and women, liturgy and sacrament brought the assurance of escape from the clutches of evil. The rhythm of worship enhanced by incense, bells, and all sorts of tactile actions yielded a holistic spirituality that engaged all the senses. Unfortunately, this same sacramental expression often broke out of the bounds of Christianity resulting in charms and incantations to ward off evil, and the veneration of shrines and relics.

In the West, this mode of worship culminated in medieval society organized around the ideal of Christendom at large. All of Western Europe and the British Isles considered themselves inheritors of the Christian faith, organized around the original concept of the Holy Roman Empire. During this time society was ordered by a divinely appointed hierarchy:

God

Kings and Pope

Lord's and Bishops

Merchants and Priests

Peasants

Non-Christians

This was seen as the natural order, appointed by God himself. One did not question their place in society, nor the authority of church and king.

The earth was the center of the universe, and mankind God's special purpose on it.

In the late medieval period, popular Christianity found expression in a variety of ways which have persisted in the Church of England even unto the present. In contrast to the word-based faith of the Reformation, medieval piety celebrated the life of faith through pictures and stories, ritual and sacrament. The appeal of this kind of spirituality should not be oversimplified, by relegating it to ignorance, or lack of education. Rather, the tenacity of medieval expressions of faith and worship points toward something deeper—an inclination within the being of mankind to worship and encounter God by means of symbols.

The common expression of Christianity at this time was picture based. The vast majority of the populace was illiterate. Only the top 2 or 3 percent had the ability to read, and the cost of books was prohibitive for all except the very wealthy. The biblical story and the doctrines of the church were enshrined in carvings and tapestries that conveyed the meanings visually. Along with these theological carvings, wall paintings and stained glass windows "taught" the laity visually and intuitively.

Medieval Christianity expressed itself with a holistic and aesthetically beautiful manner of devotional life. This expression was violently altered by the Protestant Reformation emphasis on propositional truth and austerity as a safeguard against idolatry. Yet, even though the pendulum had swung the other way, the longing of this "catholic" form of worship reemerged with the Oxford movement, and has recaptured the favor of the Anglican Communion to this day.

In our time much of what we take for granted as authentic Anglican worship would have been anathema in the Church of England during the Reformation. Vestments, candles, incense, bells, altars, banners, carvings of the Stations of the Cross, and even crucifixes all resonate with medieval Christianity. These would have been decried by the reformers as popish inventions. Yet, taken together these elements create a form of worship that is aesthetically beautiful, allowing worship from the intuitive, right brain, part of our constitution. In contrast to left-brain, analytical, linear, and propositional truth about God, the intuitive faculty within us apprehends God sacramentally, through the deep meaning contained in symbols. This truth embedded in symbol and ritual fulfills our need to know God in a personal way. The symbols that are present in our life and worship bind our hearts to that which we consider ultimately real.

There is much to be commended in the elements of late medieval piety. The holistic framework of worship engages our being in multifaceted ways. Ritual grounds our lives in the rhythm of the church year, which in turn rehearses the Christian story season after season. Story itself is commendable in conveying the truth of the gospel, because, as people, we are hardwired to think, remember, and process reality in a narrative based framework. Along with the visual and olfactory embellishments, story and drama complete the task of whole worship which music and singing begin. Thus, the affirmation of these riches in the life of medieval piety and worship has provided the Church of England with a vital strain of Christian expression primarily represented in the Anglo-Catholic quarter. Nevertheless, while most of what has been described so far presents the value, and positive aspects of this strain, there are several cautions to be considered.

The first danger in being immersed in late medieval spirituality is that ritual becomes salvation. Since the rituals or worship engage us at many levels, and are an integral part of the rhythm of life, soon they may supersede the living person of Jesus Christ as a means of salvation. Instead of trusting in the grace of God in Christ and the corresponding forgiveness of sins, one can begin to trust in the efficacy of the mass, the assurance of confession, and the joy of worship. While inviting the beauty of holiness, and affirming the benefits thereof, great care must be taken to maintain the understanding that the forms, means, and channels represent the ultimate reality of God, but are not that reality in and of themselves. The purpose, *telos*, of worship is to encounter God. In such encounter our lives are transformed, and he is glorified. The danger of ritual becoming salvation is that such encounter and transformation may never take place, the form being glorified in place of he who formed all.

Second, due to the proximity of the spiritual and material realms, and the emphasis on the conflict between the devil and God, religious life can easily slip into superstition and magic. To be clear on the definition, magic refers to the manipulation of spiritual forces to gain advantage or prevent disaster. Ritual becomes magic when it is done to thwart evil spirits, to assure prosperous business, or to enable sin without consequence. While a worldview that portrays an integration of the spiritual and material realms, as well as the conflict between good and evil, is biblical, the intent of religious life must not be to manipulate spiritual forces. Rather our intention must be to invite the presence of the Spirit and obediently align ourselves with his purposes and his power.

Finally, premodern piety embodied a right brain, intuitive, experiential expression of faith. The danger lies in this becoming unhinged from the left-brain, rational, propositional expression. The result of such an unhinging is the loss of mooring for the church. Like a sailing vessel without a rudder the church is blown about by the prevailing winds of popular sentiment—usually the one that represents the most intense experience. Without the balance of carefully reasoned doctrines and creeds we are unable to chart a certain course, and steer clear of the rocks that lie in wait to shipwreck the church. On the other hand, it should be noted that the left-brain will not function properly without the right either. Both qualities inherent in left and right are necessary to provide balance and wholeness.

The expression of late medieval piety has persisted down through history because it is closely aligned with a biblical worldview, and offers a holistic form of worship. It resonates with a part of our being often denied in modernity, but now is once again being reaffirmed in the postmodern period. Today the beauty of holiness embraced by the premodern church again speaks to the heart of postmodern men and women. Yet, to avoid the errors and excesses inherent to this right brained, experiential, expression of faith, we must provide the rudder of modern propositional understanding. The two are not mutually exclusive, but balance and enhance one another into a genuine, authentic, and whole manifestation of Christian faith.

It is important to remember that the Anglican Church was birthed in the premodern era. Christendom remained the order of the day in Western European society. To be sure, the Reformation itself was giving place to a critical evaluation of doctrines and polities, resulting in the breakup of the monolithic Roman Catholic Church. However, the reigning paradigm of the social order remained intact. The society that surrounded the Anglican Church was Christian—traditional Christian: one that upheld the authority of Holy Scripture; the authority of the church; and the authority of the monarchy. The prevailing ethics and values, the accepted norms of social discourse, were grounded in a biblical worldview—what we would call today the Judeo-Christian foundation of Western society. The Church of England had to find its way through the Catholic vs. Protestant dilemma, but it did so in a solidly Christian faith based context.

In the 1500s many of the elements which comprised the foundation of the premodern paradigm began to break down. The traditional authorities of church and king began to come into question. The long accepted hierarchy of society gave way to rising classes of merchants and craftsmen.

Anglican Manifesto

Instead of a Christendom there came the formation of nation states, unified in common language and commercial interests. Western culture was weary with the wars of religion, and longed for a new basis for human interaction and morality. Amazing breakthroughs began to take place in science and exploration, and the age of discovery was upon us. It was the age of enlightenment and reason was the light.

The Modern Paradigm

With the advent of the Enlightenment period, the social order moved forward with the paradigm shift to Modernity. Science and reason became the new authorities of the day. Nothing was beyond the razor of mankind's scintillating intellect—our critical rational power. Especially suspect were those authorities which were an integral part of the previous system of thought. The authority of tradition, the Bible, and the church were now deemed at best irrelevant, or at worst in opposition to the new order. Thus, scientific method and higher criticism were wielded as weapons designed to tear apart any perceived threat from the previous paradigm.

The achievement and honor of the individual became highly prized and valued. This was to be an age of exploration and discovery by explorers and scientists alike, with a concept of social evolution destining the exceptional for the top of society. It did not matter on which level you were born, upward mobility awaited any that could attain it. Rapid advances in technology, medicine, and understanding of the natural world resulted in an optimism which concluded that mankind could solve any and all problems given enough time and energy. In the medieval time stability and order were valued, keeping on with the way things had been. Modernity embraced change for change's sake. Change itself became a principle of operation. Rationalism, empiricism, individualism, optimism—these are the foundational values upon which the modern era was constructed.

PREMODERN	MODERN	POSTMODERN

"Because God put it there and that's the way it's always been."	"Onwards and upwards with inevitable progress!"	"Bllpppggghljsdlkfjowejfalsk djflksdjflksjdldjl;aldflkj;;;;df"

Paradigm to Paradigm

The development of the modern era witnessed a profound change in the very nature of Western society. Social norms which had been grounded in traditional modes of being, gave way to a technological reorganization that effected changes in relationships, social roles of men and women, economics, and government. The church was hard pressed to understand the dangers of this new technological era and to prepare men and women for the challenge of living a Christian life in the midst of the radical change that confronted them. The Anglican Church was not alone in grappling with the change in values brought on by the paradigm shift into the modern era. As we saw earlier, Hooker's integration of reason, along with tradition and Scripture is a prime example of theology adjusting to the context of a new paradigm.

In the nineteenth century there arose a division between science and faith, which found expression in the language of facts vs. values. This dichotomy, or schism, did not exist in the time before the Enlightenment, the premodern period, but came to exemplify the modern approach taken by both theologians and scientists alike. Upon close examination, it becomes clear that the division between science and faith is a modern construct, which overlooks the very presuppositions necessary to postulate such a view. Indeed, the biblical worldview maintains an integration of facts and values in a consistent whole. However, the modern paradigm is inconsistent, and blind to its own operating principles.

The separation between facts and values grew out of Enlightenment thinking that began with Descartes' famous axiom "I think, therefore I am." His position began the initial schism between God and man. God was no longer required to explain existence, since reason could get the job done without him. The exaltation of reason as a basis for human existence and relationship soon found a willing audience in a populace weary from the wars of religion. As the nineteenth century emerged, reason developed its own dogma of scientific investigation, supposedly objective and free of value judgments on the part of the practitioner. The scientific worldview of materialism, attempted to supplant the biblical worldview on the basis of objective vs. subjective truth. The irony of the situation is that biblical religion was in reality being challenged by a new religious philosophy—scientific materialism.

While scientific materialism claims to have its basis in objective fact, it actually embraces much on faith, and actively uses and promotes certain values. Descartes' foundational statement itself is axiomatic, that is it must be taken in faith. It cannot be "proven" scientifically that thought is the basis of existence. Reason cannot prove itself infallible, because it has no outside objective standard by which to measure itself. Reason itself is subjective, at the mercy of the values of the one who applies it. Reason was exalted in the nineteenth century because it was more highly valued by those who sought a different solution to the human predicament.

The evaluation of reason as the supreme arbiter of human affairs contributed to a corresponding devaluation of intuition. Socially this can be observed in the separation between masculine and feminine roles. Men operated in the world of facts, women in the realm of intuition and emotion. Facts were valued, and as such gained social power. In the "real" world of commerce, invention, and industrialization, facts discerned about the natural order had cash value, and produced profit for those who traded in them. The Bible, and the faith in God which it requires, was soon pulled down under the assault of relentless reason. The right-brain, feminine, intuitive side of human knowledge represented by the biblical faith, was cast aside by left-brained, masculine reason. Again, the irony is twofold: first, the scientific worldview is only possible with biblical presuppositions. One must assume an ordered, contingent universe to validate scientific endeavor. Furthermore, man's position as a being that is able to inquire into the universe and understand it, begs the question of humanity's own origin. Second, by devaluing the intuitive to a position of non-knowledge, humanity becomes fragmented, unable to integrate knowledge gained in both spheres into a constructive whole.

The integration of facts and values is precisely what is offered by the biblical worldview. While Scripture does not portend to be a manual on physics or chemistry, it nevertheless declares facts which must be wrestled with. The universe exists, and is ordered by God. As previously discussed, this fact allows the natural sciences to operate. The Bible is concerned with relationships between God and mankind, and between human beings. Its emphasis is on humanity's spiritual condition, describing the fact of sin—a hypothesis easily proven by reading any newspaper. The fact of reconciliation between God and man is the goal of biblical revelation. These facts are known existentially, being apprehended by the intuitive faculty, and affirmed and applied by reason. At the same time the Bible also presents a system of values that is derived from and supports its factual assertions. Creation is good. Humanity was fashioned in God's image; therefore human life is highly valuable. Social values provide for a right ordering of human relationships, affirming family bonds, along with generosity and compassion for others. Humility, forgiveness, giving, worship, and faith are all values derived from biblical facts. Faith itself may be both a fact and a value. The Bible presents faith as an "organ of perception" which all people exercise, a fact of human existence, and, in particular, highly values faith in God.

The modern idea that knowledge and faith are mutually exclusive flows from a set of false presuppositions regarding them both. Even scientific knowledge springs from certain axioms which must be taken by faith. Aristotle said, "We must know some things without formal proof, or argument, or we can know nothing at all." Faith is the faculty within us that allows us to apprehend first principles. Faith, reason, and intuition work together with our empirical senses and emotions, enabling us to form a comprehensive knowledge of the universe. The division of fact and values is not biblical. The Bible presents an integrated worldview in which the two are mutually interdependent. The schism between facts vs. values, left-brain vs. right-brain, masculine vs. feminine, reason vs. intuition is a modern construct arising from a particular evaluation of, and promotion of, one side over the other. As this modern construct crumbles, the reintegration of science and faith, and the affirmation of the biblical worldview becomes a possibility.

Throughout the modern era, theologians and churchmen grappled with the assault from the new secular thinking, and the new secular institutions, which challenged the veracity of Scripture and denigrated faith into a fairytale and superstition. Seeking continued relevancy, the Protestant churches in particular espoused a revised "liberal theology," which presented faith as grounded in the subjective experience of the believer. Religion was reconstituted as a social construct, one necessary for the good of humanity, reigning in the negative excesses of the desires of the individual self. In the modern era faith became an experience and religion a movement. Both were set aside from discourse in the public arena and relegated to the private sphere. It is at this time that the fracture began in the Anglican Church and by extension in Christianity at large.

While the older, traditional views continued to spread into the new Anglican churches which were growing around the world, in Africa, Asia, and South America, in the West a new liberal vision came into being. As we shall see, this liberal expression took as its starting point a very different set of presuppositions and practices than those found in the traditional biblical worldview. A new foundation for belief in God was laid by German theologians like Schleiermacher and Hegel. Their innovation was to claim subjective experience with God as holy ground, unassailable by the tenets of modernity. This vision continued to grow and develop down through the modern era of the twentieth century, with a deepening of the sense of the self as authoritative in experience with the divine. This was fused with a theological commitment to an amplified understanding of divine immanence, promoted by popular theologians like Paul Tillich. The result was an experientially oriented theological grid, which was open to direction from the surrounding culture—a ready vessel to embrace the postmodern paradigm shift.

Meanwhile the world was shrinking.

The Postmodern Paradigm

The tenets of the modern paradigm—individualism, rationalism, optimism, and innovation—lost their veracity in providing answers to the surrounding culture. Their ability to cope with the conditions and conflicts foisted upon humanity was compromised and bogged down, as countries, cultures, languages, and religions came crashing together. The next paradigm shift came due, and took us into the postmodern age, where the peoples, cultures, and religions of the world are thrown into the salad bowl together and tossed about before coming to a rest, at least temporarily, on the table of humanity. What do you like in your salad? You may chose to eat just one part, or a little bit of all.

Perhaps a salad bar is a more apt depiction of the postmodern mindset. As we walk down the line we may pick and chose from an amazing collection of ideas, lifestyles, values, practices, and beliefs, and end up with a salad made just the way we like it—slathered with our favorite dressing on top. And, please, make no critical evaluation of the person's salad next to you in line. That is not acceptable, mind your manners!

Pluralism in the Postmodern Era

As we near the end of the twentieth century, historians and scholars recognize that another paradigm shift has taken place. We have left the modern age and entered into what is called the postmodern era. This new era is characterized by radical religious and ideological pluralism, an information explosion, the relativity of truth, and the creation of individual realities. The net result of these phenomena is a seething social cauldron which periodically boils over with alarming results.

Pluralism, defined as various religious, cultural, and ideological expressions, has always been present, de facto, in the world. Throughout human history vast empires and cultures have developed dramatically different worldviews. However, until recently these worldviews have been practically isolated from one another by virtue of the sheer distances that separated them.

With the advent of the modern age the world began to shrink at a pace that defied the imagination. Within two hundred years, 1790–1990, technology advanced the discovering and linking together of one culture to another more than in all the millenniums prior. In many ways the conflicts and wars of the modern era reflect the friction and tensions resulting from the sudden juxtaposition of religious, philosophical, and sociological ideologies. The net result of this process is what has come to be called the "Global Village."

Anglican Manifesto

We now live in a world that is linked by instant communication and, relatively speaking, lightening fast transportation. Ideas and money can be transferred around the globe virtually in an instant. Western technology and ideology has gone forth to conquer the world, and with it Christianity longing to fulfill the Great Commission of Jesus. Conversely the religious beliefs and philosophies of the East have come back to find a new homeland in Western civilization. Speaking from the Western perspective and as a Christian, I think we have been caught by surprise.

The West has had a developing history of religious pluralism from the time of the Reformation. The schismatic quality of Protestantism spawned, and continues to spawn, an ever increasing set of religious persuasions; however, all of these, from the Roman Catholic Church to the charismatic movement, hold to the basic belief of the truth embodied in Jesus Christ. Now in the present, there is a sudden explosion of religious thought that holds the truth to be something other than Christ.

In a discussion of truth there are only two options. The first is that truth is objective and is and of itself a standard to be understood, or apprehended. The other option is that truth is relative; it is subjective and to be determined by the individual or society as they think best. As beauty is in the eye of the beholder, truth is in the mind of the thinker (or perhaps the heart of the feeler). In the premodern era truth was objective, then came the modern era and resulting conflicts. Now in the postmodern era, truth has become relative as an attempt is being made to mitigate the radical differences in which we find ourselves in the midst of in the Global Village.

In our abandonment of objective truth, we now find ourselves in a world of competing relative truths. Anyone can establish anything as a truth claim and thereby gain power in correlation to their ability to persuade others of the validity of that claim. Truth is what you can persuade others to believe. Although most systems of truth have roots in various religious expressions from the modern, premodern, or even ancient ages, there is no idiom within society to prevent the invention of, or synthesizing of new religious movements. This process is known as syncretism, and continues to be very active and popular in our time.

The question for the Christian in all of this is: "Where is Christ?" Jesus said, "I am the way, the truth and the life, no one comes to the Father except through me" (John 14:6). This statement defined church dogma until the advance of uncertainty in the modern era. As other religions have contended with Christianity, Christians have met people of other faiths who exhibit Christ-likeness without naming the name of Jesus. In some cases pious Muslims, Hindus, Buddhists, etc. may have a better witness of integrity and morality than the Christian church. As a result Christian theologians have been jumping through hoops to try to reconcile the paradoxes that they are being confronted with.

One solution is inclusive theology which keeps Christ as the Savior but transforms judgment to a proximal basis. While Christ is the truth for all men/women, each individual is only accountable for responding to the amount of truth found in their particular religion or culture. This solution seems to borrow heavily from the Hindu concept that all paths lead to God. Furthermore, inclusive theology does not negate the very real differences in the conception of God: personal vs. impersonal, real vs. abstract, eternal vs. temporal, and human vs. divine.

As Christians we must realize that we do not have an exclusive package of truth, but that other religions do indeed have elements of truth within them. The difference is that Christianity has Christ, the Savior, and that he has appeared once for the salvation of all. This of course throws us back to the premodern stance, and this I believe is where Christians need to ground themselves. As C. S. Lewis declared, Christ was either a liar, a lunatic, or who he said he was, the Lord of Heaven and Earth.[1] If we change him in order to fit a postmodern paradigm that promotes many ways to God, then we have in fact eliminated the biblical Jesus Christ altogether. Instead, we are left with a modified Christ of our own construction; one which will be much more accepted and less confrontational, but, one who is in fact not the person of Jesus Christ.

Where is the postmodern world headed? With the rise of new religious movements and the dissimilation of the previously existing structures, pieces of religious ideology and practice are being scattered everywhere. Eager practitioners gather up the fragments to form their own versions which gain strength as seekers become adherents. Greater multitudes of religious diversity are being dissimilated over an ever increasing area. The gatherer-seeker idiom is becoming pervasive throughout our society. In turn each new group exerts power and influence in an attempt to outgrow the others and thereby establish its dominion as the one truth.

Like so many hatchlings in the West competing for the worm, the facets of radical pluralism compete for humanity. In reality how many of these can ultimately survive? The weaker birds are pushed out of the nest to make

---

1. See Lewis, *Mere Christianity*, 56.

room for the stronger. This Nietzschean outlook presupposes that power is the element binding our pluralistic society together. The only way out of postmodernity is the emergence of a powerful unified whole which brings together truth out of it's places of capture within the diversity surrounding us, or else total social disintegration where no faction can overcome the others and competition becomes fanatic—i.e., Bosnia, Rwanda, or more currently Syria.

As a counterbalance to the power struggle that comes as a natural outgrowth of pluralism, the postmodern era has embraced tolerance as another preeminent value. Tolerance attempts to disconnect competing systems of belief from striving with one another. Let's take the fighters out of the ring, and all sit down and have a cup of tea together. Your way is right for you. My way is right for me. It is not necessary for us to convince one another, or try to undermine one another. Instead, let us be tolerant, disengaged from the fight and all will be well. The promotion of tolerance as a vital part of postmodern morality cannot be understated. How else can we save ourselves from the wars of religion that are coming in the twenty-first century? The problem of course is that tolerance very quickly becomes intolerance when anyone attempts a truth claim that is construed as universal. "Marriage is designed by God to be between one man and one woman." Run for your life! This kind of thought will not be tolerated. Tolerance then becomes yet another means of persuasion, used to disarm the competition until my view can prevail. Remember postmodern truth is what you can persuade others to believe. Nowhere can this be seen more clearly than in the workings of the Anglican Communion as a whole. Again, Anglican-Ism seems to find itself in the middle of it all.

Pluralism has leapt out of history to become a defining value of the postmodern age. Relativism and tolerance join in the new value system, promising liberation and squelching opposition. The rapid transference of ideas, money, and people made possible by the advance of technology promise quantitative and qualitative increase in the intensity of pluralistic exchange. Societies, and indeed, civilization itself, hang in the balance as they grapple with emerging problems, conflicts, and partial solutions. Yet, even as we have begun to come to terms with the dynamics of what has come to be known as postmodernity, another historical paradigm shift has already begun to take place beneath our feet.

Paradigm to Paradigm

The Oneworld Era

Turning into the twenty-first century, postmodernity itself is beginning to show signs of disintegration, as a new paradigm is emerging. For my purposes, I have named this new time period the oneworld era. I think most would agree this is exactly what we are dealing with. This next paradigm shift is under way even as I write. The salad buffet of the postmodern era is being put into the blender, turned into cream of vegetable soup, and served hot and steaming to a world that is bound together as one. As we conclude this reflection on the Anglican Church in relation to the historical paradigms shifts in the West, let us now consider the signs and evidence of the new oneworld paradigm which is in formation all around us.

The evidence for a shift out of the postmodern era into a new paradigm is mounting. This new oneworld era is seen first in the economic realities and challenges which are now taking place in the world. Countries no longer have independent control over their own economies. All nations are already linked together in a de facto oneworld economy. When the United States economy goes into recession, it affects Europe, which in turn affects the third world. China, India, Brazil, and Russia are up-and-coming economic powerhouses, but the interdependence of them all with the rest of the world cannot be denied: "When a butterfly flaps its wings in Beijing, it rains in Detroit"; "When the United States sneezes, the world catches cold." Thus, the very dynamics of the time we live in are putting pressure on all to bring productivity, labor, trade, and currency into some kind of unified system. The systems currently running in old paradigm mode will at some point be unable to keep the pace, resulting in crisis, creative destruction, and replacement with the new.

Not only is the world ever increasingly linked together economically, but in several other ways as well. Ecologically we are all sharing the same finite planet. Concerns for global warming, pollution controls, over-fishing international waters, genetic engineering of the food supply, and the green movement in general show oneworld thinking and actions that are increasingly taking center stage. Communication is now instant around the globe. That means that the sharing of ideas, attitudes, and relationships is also now instant. Humanity is connected. Humanity is in relationship with itself. No matter where you may happen to find yourself on the planet no longer are you separate from the whole. The concept of being a citizen of the world is emerging and gaining strength and credibility. Think globally act locally.

So, what remains to complete a oneworld paradigm? First, we have yet to witness a political solution that transcends the nation states, bringing all into a worldwide government. This may not be as farfetched, nor as far away at one may think. Historically, governments and empires come and go; to believe that we are somehow immune from this process is somewhat naïve. Also required for the new oneworld era, and of special importance to us as Christians, is the emergence of a Oneworld Religion. As the radicalization of the tenets of modernity resulted in the paradigm shift to the postmodern era, so to the radicalization of tenets of postmodernity pluralism will result in a fusion into one religious system: pluralism dictates that all religions be treated as valid and equal, the logical conclusion is a unified religion which synchronizes all into a harmony of faith; monism provides the new theological ideal of religions all worshipping the same divine force according to their cultural formation; relativism and tolerance will call for the celebration of all, not as distinct from one another, but as a multifaceted jewel—all parts of the whole; finally, the fear of religious conflicts and wars, and perhaps radical Islam, will drive even the desire of atheists to find an amenable solution.

The principle of a oneworld religion is already the desire of many, and the syncretism needed to produce such a faith is at work in the spirit of the age that surrounds us. The liberal vision of the Episcopal Church and other mainstream Protestant churches, combined with a similar impetus in the various religions, could soon produce such a oneworld religion. One need simply review the work of the United Religions Initiative sponsored by the Episcopal Church to see the progress being made. Traditional Anglicans, and Christians, will find themselves at odds with this development, because to fit Christianity into the mold essential doctrines will need to be changed. In particular, Jesus has to be changed in order to fit in. This is in fact exactly what is happening, and why the Anglican Church is in crisis.

On the positive side, the fires that are forging the new oneworld era are also purifying the faithful believers in Jesus Christ across denominational lines. A great dividing is taking place between those who are taking the path dictated by the spirit of the age, and those committed to the faith once delivered to the saints. The pressure to conform to the dictates of the new oneworld religious movement is resulting in Christians everywhere making a fresh commitment to the essential doctrines of the faith. Taken together, momentum is building for the unification of the Christian church in a way not seen since its beginning. The dividing walls are coming down, as churches found across the spectrum of genuine Christianity realize that they believe in the same truth of the gospel, and that truth is under attack. In conclusion, I believe the emerging Oneworld Religion will find itself in conflict with an equally emerging Oneworld Church, comprised of a unified fellowship of Christians of all denominations who hold to the traditional doctrines and practice of the faith.

Throughout the paradigm shifts of Western society the Anglican-Ism has survived, giving place to these distinct expressions of faith and practice: liberal, evangelical, catholic, and charismatic. Due to their adherence to the traditional authorities of the premodern era, and their acceptance of the biblical worldview in general, the latter three can be included together under the heading of conservative, or orthodox. In living through the paradigm shift to postmodernity in the West, the conservative camp has continued to diminish both in size and influence, especially in the United States and Canada. Meanwhile, the liberal faction has taken hold of the reins of power, setting their theology and practice to join with the spirit of the age in expanding the postmodern worldview. Albeit, conflict is on the horizon as the conservative expressions found largely in the newly formed Anglican Global South churches are thriving, and have, over time, matured into a force to be reckoned with.

Pluralism, relativism, and tolerance were the new authorities of the postmodern era. In many ways, these represent the ideals of modernity, radicalized, and taken to their logical conclusion. As we find ourselves immersed in the next paradigm shift, Anglican-Ism produces not one clear vision, but in reality two competing visions of what it means to be the church. This visions are growing distinct and organized, visible in the faith communities which embrace, promote and develop them. (1) A liberal postmodern vision authorized by the subjective experience of the self with the Divine, and found mainly in the progressive churches in the West; (2) A conservative orthodox vision authorized by an objective reading of Holy Scripture and visible in the evangelical, Anglo-Catholic, and charismatic churches of the Global South. Finally, the Anglican-Ism has come to the crossroads, where simply reasserting that we are all one church because we all share a Book of Common Prayer (BCP) will no longer suffice. Indeed, even the commonality of the BCP is challenged by the emergence of new liturgies, which promote theologies further and further afield from a traditional Christian belief.

Anglican Manifesto

It is the comprehensiveness, openness, and vitality of the Anglican-Ism that gave rise to this liberal/conservative dichotomy. It is the lack of boundaries and absence of central authority, the high value of autonomy, also found in the mix, which have now created the dilemma we find ourselves in. Which worldview will prevail in the contest for the soul of Anglicanism? This question is particularly acute for conservatives, who although in the majority worldwide, have been unable to secure the communion against liberal innovations. Meanwhile, liberals steadily beat the drum of revision, with a commitment to see their will accomplished and a patient strategy designed to wear down their opponents and win the day.

Paradigm to paradigm the Anglican Church has come down through history. The flexibility and resilience of the Anglican-Ism has brought us this far, only to come at last to crisis. It is a crisis that is formulated on the cusp of the next paradigm shift to the oneworld era. It is a crisis that must be resolved, that will be resolved one way or another. It is a crisis of two visions: each with its own theology; each with its own practice; each with its own agenda.

Oil and water will not mix, as we shall see in the next chapter.

Two paths diverged in a wood.
I took the path less traveled by, and that made all the difference.

—ROBERT FROST

3
Two Visions

As we follow the Anglican Church down through the paradigm shifts of history, we can readily observe the development of two separate and distinct visions, each striving for ascendancy. Both seek to answer the question, "What does it mean to be a Christian?" Each promotes its own set of answers, theological beliefs, and accepted practices. One of these visions can be identified as Liberal Protestant Christianity and is commonly called progressive. The other vision is most often referred to as conservative, or orthodox Christianity, and would consider itself to be apostolic—that is, holding to the original teachings of the apostles.

These two visions are both viable and visible within Anglican-Ism, but are by no means limited to the Anglican Church. To the contrary, both are actively being embraced and practiced by congregations and denominations across the whole spectrum of the church universal. Indeed, in our time there has emerged a great competition for the heart and soul of

Christendom, and many are beginning to awake to this fact. The question is, "What can be done?"

Every vision springs forth from basic first principles or assumptions about what is real, true, or vitally important. These are found in what are commonly called worldviews. Worldviews give "axiomatic," first answers to the essential questions which confront us in life. Questions such as: Why are we here? What is the nature of reality? Is there a God? What happens in death? How do we decide right from wrong? Worldviews comprise the foundation upon which a vision is built. Once vision is brought into being, it further influences our perception of what we see and understand. An operating system develops from the lines of code beneath that directs the ideas and practices we are actively engaged in, along with the desire to perpetuate or develop them as time unfolds.

Before we can move forward toward proposal of action, first let us take time to bring each vision into sharper focus. In this manner we will be able to better ascertain the distinctions between them, the ways in which they contradict one another, and the inherent conflict that comes from both claiming legitimacy. In doing so we will discover that in our time it is no longer sufficient to simply say, "I am a Christian." We must now go further, much further, in explaining what we mean when we say it.

Origins of the Liberal Vision

To begin our consideration of how these two visions came into being, let us take a step back to the period of the Enlightenment, a time of transition into the modern era. This is when reason had emerged as the reigning value for mankind, after the bloody wars between Roman Catholic and Protestant religions had left Europe longing for a more sensible way to order society.

During this time the traditional authority vested in the Holy Scriptures and the church lost credibility, and were challenged by a rising objective secularism in the universities, which took the form of an activity know as higher criticism. In response, and perhaps also in participation, a prominent group of German theologians sought to move the residency of Christian faith onto a different foundation—one that could withstand the assault of unbridled reason; one that allowed for modern sensibilities; and one that embraced and affirmed the deeper meanings of our humanity. Chief among these theologians was Friedrich Schleiermacher.

Schleiermacher comes into prominence as a modern theologian in Germany. He was educated in the Moravian school of German Pietist, and as a young man was confronted with a general disdain for religion among his peers. Religion had come to be despised by the educated classes in Germany, with Christianity in particular being discredited by German scholars as historically suspect and scientifically untrue. Schleiermacher sought to answer these critiques and set religion on a new foundation, one that was impervious from attack by the Enlightenment weapons of reason, facts, and knowledge based on scientific method.

At this time romanticism had come into vogue as a reaction to what many perceived as a dehumanizing cold rationality, which had taken over as the governing paradigm of society. Romantics rediscovered and idealized nature, and man's interaction with it. In turning from the analytical left-brain world of facts and science, a renaissance of art, music, poetry—right brain creativity and intuition—flourished as people sought to perceive the inner essence of human existence. Feeling and intuition were highly valued, along with the experience of the individual.

In this highly affective environment, Schleiermacher crafted his apology for a more acceptable Christianity in his *Speeches on Religion to Its Cultured Despisers*, which based religion in an existential expression of feelings and experience. He drew a sharp distinction between the realm of the intellect, science and knowledge, and the realm of faith, feeling and intuition. For Schleiermacher faith constituted another form of knowing, which touched on the divine in ways not possible by the rational side of our being. Feeling is much more than a passing emotional moment. It is an experience of connection with divine consciousness.

In expressing his idea of God, or the Divine, Schleiermacher uses many different terms: the Infinite, the Whole, Nature, Universe, Universal Lawgiver, the Eternal, etc. It is of note that none of these monikers convey a classic theistic concept of God as a personal being—i.e., Father, Son, Holy Spirit. Instead the concept of the Divine takes on a non-personal quality, a deeper consciousness which we all experience through and in the universe. This experience, along with the feeling of dependence on something greater than ourselves, combines to form the basis of religion. He writes that religion is essentially contemplative: "The contemplation of the pious in the immediate consciousness of the universal existence of all finite things in and through the Infinite, all temporal things in and through the Eternal."[1]

---

1. Schleiermacher, *Speeches on Religion*, 36–37.

Therefore, the various outward forms of religion—doctrine, dogma, or ritual—are merely human attempts to formalize the experience of the Infinite that is common to all. Religion is not found through knowledge in the rational sense of the word. Rather it comes to us as a deep feeling—a revelation of the Infinite in the finite. Schleiermacher grounds religion and Christianity in the inner essence, the kernel of human affect, experienced by each person in their own particular individuality. This experience then gives rise to the various corporate expressions of religion, which act as portals to the deeper truth for the novice. The whole of religion only being possible when viewed through an endless number of forms which must encapsulate every person's experience.[2]

Schleiermacher is considered to be the father of liberalism, and rightly so. By basing theology in the personal experience of the individual, he paved the way for the development of modern liberalism in which the essence of religion is subjective, rather than objective. Revelation is changed from an historical event to an immediate experience. Liberalism emphasizes that we can find God within ourselves, and that the divine kingdom can be identified in the historical process. We find God in the evolutionary process of nature and history, not in the creeds and sacraments of the Church.

Liberalism paints an optimistic picture of the human condition and of history. Since religion is grounded in a subjective experience common to all people, universalism is the logical conclusion. Liberal theology has a powerful appeal to modern mankind as it affirms the validity of all religions and maintains the autonomy of every individual. The dictum of "God within" frees every man and woman from any obligation to objective standards of religious dogma; all are at liberty to define what is right in their own eyes. There is no need to repent and receive forgiveness, as sin is more of a "troubled harmony within ourselves" which destroys our relationship with the divine. Thus, universal acceptance and love of self promote the optimistic growth of human potential in an ever upward spiral of evolution.

In the present there are many expressions of religion which resonate with Schleiermacher and the liberal stream. Some are Christian, or rather called such, others are not. Schleiermacher changes the nature of Christian religion from objective worship of a transcendent God to subjective experience of Divine immanence. In doing so he set the stage for a religious expression that is monistic, rather than theistic.

Monism, the belief that God the Divine is the essence, or kernel of all that exists, is a belief commonly held by many of the world's major religions,

2. See Schleiermacher, *Speeches on Religion*, 211.

such as Hinduism and Buddhism, as well as the so called "New Age" religion common in the West. New Age is often a broad term used to describe an eclectic religious expression based on monistic principles. In all these various manifestations, including liberal Protestantism, the experience of the self in the quest for the feeling of oneness with the divine is the apex of religion. Schleiermacher writes, "The soul is dissolved in the immediate feeling of the infinite and eternal."[3]

Let me express some sympathy for Friedrich Schleiermacher, and place some of his theology in a different light. To begin we should understand the context in which he lived was antithetical to any idea of the validity of religion. By establishing faith as part of the intuitive realm of human existence, Schleiermacher provided an important corrective to the cold rationalism of the Enlightenment. Certainly many of his tenets are valid observations of religious life. There is a place for the subjective experience of an individual's encounter with God, and feeling can be a true way of knowing. The problem develops when the intuitive feeling side of our being becomes all that can inform us. By jettisoning the rational, objective side of our makeup as part of religion, we open the dichotomy between transcendent and immanent, leaving us with no transcendent reality to guide or correct us. How can we then give meaning to mystical experience and history itself? Schleiermacher fell into the schism between left-brain rationalism and right-brain intuition and as a result lost the whole knowledge of God, which comes through a composite of both. To maintain the integrity of Christian faith we must integrate our understanding of God's transcendence with his immanence—the objective historical reality with the subjective immediate reality. Only then can we avoid the pitfall of romanticism, which diverted Schleiermacher and those who followed after him.

Conservative Responses

In some ways the identification of the beginning of the liberal vision is easier to describe than the conservative vision. This is because the current version of progressive Christianity is clearly a development from the modern era going forward. In contrast, conservative Christianity would look for its roots all the way back to the early church. Naturally so, since this is the inherent meaning of conservative—to conserve what came before or to keep intact the deposit that has been given.

3. Schleiermacher, *Speeches on Religion*, 17.

Anglican Manifesto

Conservative Christianity draws its strength from the early councils of the church, which by and large defined orthodox theological beliefs and practices over against false variations and heresies of the time. Deference to the apostles and the Holy Scriptures, taken as inspired in the plain meaning of the text, combined to reinforce the strength of the creeds brought into being through the early councils of the whole church. Church fathers and theologians, such as Augustine of Hippo, Basil the Great, and Thomas Aquinas, contributed further insights to the vision according to their time. Many newer church expressions today, who in fact embody and promote a conservative vision of Christianity, might do well to remember that for centuries the Roman Catholic and Eastern Orthodox expressions kept trust for future generations.

But what about the conservative vision during the modern period when the liberal counterpart emerged? How has the conservative vision developed in the time from modernity forward?

As we have seen, the development of liberal theology came in many ways as a response to the attacks from modern critical thinking. Belief in the Bible, the hierarchy of the church, and the teachings of the church fathers were being ripped to shreds during the time of the Enlightenment by secular scholars who developed a method known as higher criticism. In the rush to reason and scientific method as the new arbiters of objective truth, ancient authorities were cast aside. This included church offices, creeds, and councils, as well as the Bible. Like their liberal counterparts, conservatives also grappled with these challenges and reacted in ways that were not that unpredictable.

In many ways conservative Christianity began to withdraw from the public sphere. With its credibility threatened, while being castigated in the public sectors of science, commerce, and education, conservatives battened down the hatches within their respective communities. In some cases they proceeded in forming their own Bible colleges to counter the secular universities. Fundamentalism emerged as a kind of fortress against the assault. Once again conserving, keeping intact, the foundational truths of what it means to be a Christian.

At times revivals broke out in a type of counter offensive, bringing many to faith in Jesus Christ in the same manner and understanding known down through time. The older Christian expressions of Roman Catholic and Eastern Orthodox remained consistent through this time as well, and new movements that emphasized the gifts of the Holy Spirit, the charismata, exploded on the scene at the turn of the twentieth century. Ironically, this charismatic expression of Christianity also turned to an experience of God as essential, valid, and unassailable by the world. Yet, charismatics by and large remained anchored in the basic principles of the conservative vision, whereas the liberals cut the rope and set the sails on a new course.

Schleiermacher and company had captivated the Protestant stream with a vision of God within, diverting the flow in a new direction. Most of this school of German theologians joined with him, but there was one who stood against the tide. Karl Barth was saturated with liberal theology in his training, and found it wanting. In response he wrote a commentary on Paul's Epistle to the Romans, reasserting the traditional beliefs of the Christian faith. It was said by the press at the time that Barth's book fell like a bombshell on the playground of liberal theology, with the added shock value being that Barth was one of their own. Barth declared that God cannot be reduced to the realm of subjective human experience. He is beyond, transcendent, wholly other. God initiates contact with humanity on his own terms, through his mighty acts in history. Actions exemplified in the coming of Jesus Christ.

Barth is an example of a theologian that continued the conservative vision, and gave to it the insights needed for his time. His massive work, *Church Dogmatics*, expounds on the basic doctrines and beliefs held by the Christian church for thousands of years. His conservative stance earned him the title "neo-orthodox"—orthodox in the new modern era. He along with others kept the conservative candle lit on the windowsill of the Protestant churches, providing a steadfast critique against the prevalent liberalism of the day. This critique is summed up by Richard Niebuhr, who continued in Barth's path of neo-orthodoxy in standing against the social gospel of the mid twentieth century: "A God without wrath brought man without sin into a kingdom without judgment through the ministration of a Christ without a cross."[4]

Evangelicals also had their part to play in the continuance of the conservative vision, with resurgence worthy of John Wesley. Billy Graham and his crusade proclaimed the gospel around the United States, and eventually the world. Evangelical colleges, such as Wheaton, Biola, and Westmont, were formed to provide scholarly education which also affirmed faith and belief in the Bible. The evangelical movement came home in the Anglican Church through the ministries of the likes of John Stott and J. I. Packer.

---

4. Niebuhr, *Kingdom of God in America*, 193.

In time Trinity Episcopal School for Ministry was formed in the United States in order to provide theological training grounded in the evangelical/conservative way of belief.

Packer portrays evangelicals as the standard bearers of orthodoxy in the Anglican Church. This is an awesome responsibility, one that carries with it the challenge to confront heretical viewpoints as being unchristian. By recognizing the unity which evangelicals have by means of agreement on the essentials, a solid base for identity can be maintained in the face of such challenges. Above all the seduction of pluralism, under the guise of tolerance, should be avoided by maintaining the uniqueness of Christ and the necessity of the gospel.

Evangelicalism is grounded on a cluster of six controlling convictions, each of which is regarded as being true, of vital importance, and grounded in Scripture. These are not purely doctrinal, if this term is understood to refer solely to a set of objective truths; they are also existential, in that they affirm the manner in which the believer is caught up in a redemptive and experiential encounter with the living Christ. These six fundamental convictions can be set out as follows:

Six Evangelical Fundamentals

1. The Supremacy of Holy Scripture

   —*the source of knowledge of God and a guide to Christian living*

2. The Majesty of Jesus Christ

   —*both as incarnate God and Lord and as the Savior of sinful humanity*

3. The Lordship of the Holy Spirit

   —*third person of the Trinity who guides us in all truth*

4. The Necessity of Conversion

   —*personal decision to accept Christ as Savior*

5. The Priority of Evangelism

   —*for both individual Christians and the church as a whole*

6. The Importance of Fellowship

   —*Christian community is vital for spiritual nourishment, fellowship and growth*[5]

---

5. McGrath, "Evangelical Distinctives," 55–56.

Evangelical is a term by which a rather broad section of the church would identify itself with today, especially in the West. While forms of worship may vary between contemporary and traditional styles, and doctrines may differ, the Six Evangelical Fundamentals are a set of core beliefs. Agreement on these fundamental tenets of the faith unites Anglican evangelicals with those in other denominations, promoting a value of ecumenical unity. At the risk of over simplification, evangelicals claim faithfulness to apostolic teaching as the criteria by which to judge an authentic expression of the church.

And so, the conservative vision has remained viable in the Anglican Church and throughout worldwide Christianity. While all the while alongside, the liberal vision has grown in strength, character, and adherents. As we come to the second half of the twentieth century, both begin to crystallize in their assertion of what it means to be a Christian: liberals by adapting to the contemporary culture around them; conservatives reasserting truth from the past.

The Liberal Vision Refined

In the West, the Anglican/Episcopal Church has maintained an elite social status. The ideology of the culture reaffirmed the theologically liberal presuppositions flowing from the post-enlightenment modern era. Church and culture began a dance of affirmation, informing one another while propagating a progressive view of God and human nature. A good example is Episcopal Bishop John Robinson's book *Honest to God*, written in the nineteen sixties. In it he encapsulates a modern critical approach to Scripture, and asserts the desirability of redefining, or revising, the doctrines of the Christian faith.

Robinson seeks to express a progressive Christianity that is at one with the surrounding culture. His book is a synthesis of the presuppositions of the Enlightenment, Romanticism, and the reductionist ethics of liberal Protestantism. He embraces the tenets of secular humanism, and infuses them with a wholly immanent concept of God, in order to produce a worldview that is best described as monistic. Authority is transferred to the autonomous self in opposition to the tradition of church and state. Optimism reigns supreme in the ability of human achievement and understanding. As Robinson quotes throughout his book, "Man has come of age."[6]

6. Robinson, *Honest to God*.

Robinson draws heavily from the thought of Rudolf Bultmann, who attempted to rescue the truth of Scripture by "demythologizing" it. Supernatural aspects of Scripture were scientifically impossible, and thus no longer credible to modern man. Yet, within these myths lay valuable insights that could be reclaimed, the so called kernel within the husk, or *kerygma*. Christian faith must shed its traditional cocoon and metamorphosize into a new, more advanced state, one that is more in league with mankind in the twentieth century. He applies an evolutionary model to Christianity, demonstrating how the supernatural aspects of Scripture were the only conceptual devices available to "primitive man" as means of describing their encounter with God, and the life of Jesus Christ. He bases his "reluctant revolution" of the present, on the previous transformation in thought from a God up there, in a three-tiered universe, to a God "out there" in Enlightenment times. Moderns, he asserts, can no longer believe in this kind of God. Rather, God is to be found within, through the experience of personal relationships.

Robinson promotes a radical revision of Christian theology, expounding on Tillich's vision of God as the immanent Ground of all Being. God is no longer a person "out there," rather God is the essence of being that undergirds all life. This God is known not through the worship of religion, nor through personal asceticism, but by means of the experience of personal relationship. God is love, and love can only be known in the giving of ourselves to others. Thus, we touch and "feel God, the unconditional, only in personal experience, the conditional." Robinson asserts that this is what the New Testament writers were trying to describe by depicting God as a person. Yet, now this myth must yield its deeper truth of the God within.[7]

God is not known in the heights as a transcendent creator; God is experienced in the depths, a pure immanence that is at one with creation. Robinson rehabilitates the understanding of transcendence by subordinating it to immanence. The depths of the Ground of all Being are fathomless. We can only hope to experience the surface waters, like a snorkeler diving in the midst of the deep sea. This bottomless Being is so beyond our comprehension that it transcends all human consciousness. Immanence is transcendent. Furthermore, naturalism acknowledges this Being as present by demonstrating evidence of the creative power of nature. The Ground of all Being is the deep undercurrent of all life, creatively evolving higher and

---

7. See Robinson, *Honest to God*, chap 3, "The Ground of All Being."

higher forms of consciousness. This understanding may be best described as panentheism.

All theology is anthropology, for God is within us and known only in knowing ourselves. Therefore, "theological affirmations are in reality assertions about human existence," albeit "about the ultimate depth and ground of that existence."[8]

In light of this understanding Robinson redefines the concepts of God found in the traditional Christian myth. Since God is not a person, the attributes of God are separated from his being and applied to humanity. Human experience becomes ultimate. Omnipresence and Omniscience are qualities found within human beings. The Spirit refers to a deep level of being and perception, while the flesh connotes shallowness. This brings us to the one who attained ultimate depth—Jesus Christ.

Robinson begins his interpretation, or reinterpretation, of Christ from the promise that Jesus never actually claimed to be God. He cites Tillich in describing Jesus as the man who was completely united with the Ground of all Being. As stated earlier this being is love, and the union with love is only experienced in living for others. This is what Jesus did. He was a "Man for Others," living the totality of his life in the depths of love. The divine nature of Christ springs from his spirit, the deep level of perception of God within. The traditional concept of the incarnation is rejected by Robinson, as part of the antiquated myth of the early church.

Jesus was simply a man who lived out of the Ground of all Being, giving himself totally for others in love. Yet, in order to be completely united with God, it was necessary to empty himself in the final act of sacrifice on the cross. On the cross all separation was eliminated and Jesus became one with God. Thus, he became the Christ, the "medium of final revelation." Christ then becomes the apogee of human consciousness, the divine example for us to follow. In a sense, one could say that the being of Jesus merged with the Being within all reality in much the same way that Buddha was enlightened and entered nirvana, becoming one with the Void. Robinson incorporates resurrection and atonement in a concept of Christ that is a new modality of existence.

Having established a new paradigm for God and Christ, Robinson elucidates the consequences of his thinking upon worship, morality, and Christianity in general. He continues to operate from the premise that traditional Christianity is wedded to a supra-naturalist worldview, which is

---

8. Robinson, *Honest to God*, 52.

now obsolete and incredible. To "save" the gospel it must be extracted and "recast" into a new form that people who have "come of age" can accept. Worship, especially the Eucharist and liturgy, take on new significance as the conduit to the divine Being within. Christ, the new modality of being, is manifest where love is experience through personal relationships. Likewise, love is the standard of all morality. Nothing can be determined to be right or wrong by any objective method, each situation must be intuitively judged by love from within. Thus, situation ethics alone are validated.

God as the Ground of all Being is the foundation for all that exists, with no differentiation between the secular and the religious. In fact, religious life, while serving for a time as a vessel for the truth, has outlived its purpose and has now become a hindrance. The Ground is to be known more through the secular experience than through the religious one. We must be willing to "discard every image of God to get to ultimate reality." In effect Robinson posits a radical reimaging of God. He appeals to the pride and arrogance of modern man, who has exalted human reason to the position of being final arbiter of all truth. The God in the depths of our being soon becomes the God of our being, then we become God.

By embracing the presuppositions of the Enlightenment, Robinson embraces a new worldview. One that is distinctly different from the biblical worldview, and the heart beat of traditional Christianity. He promotes a monistic, or panentheistic, theology in opposition to the classic distinction between God and creation. He dismantles traditional Christianity, redefining its core components and impregnating them with new meaning. In doing so he retains traditional language and incorporates it into a radically different system of belief.

We have spent some time with John Robinson because he is a pivotal figure who represents the culmination of the liberal vision that began in modernity. *Honest to God* was written on the cusp of the paradigm shift to the postmodern era, and serves as a springboard for those who follow. Continuing the trajectory, others, such as Sallie MacFague and Bishop John Shelby Spong, took the next steps in delivering a revised Christianity made ready and pliable for acceptance into an emerging postmodern ethos.

MacFague draws upon previous uses of mother imagery for God in the writings of female Christian mystics during medieval times and, surprisingly, from insights garnished from Near Eastern goddess religions to make her case that God as Mother is a historically valid portrayal. Furthermore, she portrays the Motherhood of God as a metaphor more viably suited for the contemporary sensibility.

The interrelatedness of all life, including God, is the goal to which MacFague aspires. Mother God gives and participates in the life of the world, whereas Father God stands aloof and intervenes only in the process of redemption. "The uneasy feeling many Protestants have about God as the 'ground of all Being' arises from the fact that their consciousness is shaped by the demanding father image for which righteousness and not the gift of life is primary. What the father-God gives is redemption from sins; what the mother-God gives is life."[9]

The portrait of God as Mother, who gives birth to and nurtures the world, effectively establishes a monistic doctrine of God's nature. God and the world are indistinct from one another, creation itself being part of God. All of the created order and God are interdependent, one does not exist without the other. MacFague describes the world as being God's body, in a manner best represented as panentheistic. Thus, her theological depiction of creation is radically altered from the traditional understanding.

This revision is clearly in view when the now Episcopal presiding bishop, Katherine Jeffry Schori, prayed to "Mother Jesus" immediately following her consecration.

And finally, Bishop Spong shreds Christianity completely with his Twelve Theses:

1. Theism, as a way of defining God, is dead. So most theological God-talk is today meaningless. A new way to speak of God must be found.

2. Since God can no longer be conceived in theistic terms, it becomes nonsensical to seek to understand Jesus as the incarnation of the theistic deity. So the Christology of the ages is bankrupt.

3. The biblical story of the perfect and finished creation from which human beings fell into sin is pre-Darwinian mythology and post-Darwinian nonsense.

4. The virgin birth, understood as literal biology, makes Christ's divinity, as traditionally understood, impossible.

5. The miracle stories of the New Testament can no longer be interpreted in a post-Newtonian world as supernatural events performed by an incarnate deity.

---

9. MacFague, *Models for God*, 101.

Anglican Manifesto

6. The view of the cross as the sacrifice for the sins of the world is a barbarian idea based on primitive concepts of God and must be dismissed.

7. Resurrection is an action of God. Jesus was raised into the meaning of God. It therefore cannot be a physical resuscitation occurring inside human history.

8. The story of the Ascension assumed a three-tiered universe and is therefore not capable of being translated into the concepts of a post-Copernican space age.

9. There is no external, objective, revealed standard writ in Scripture or on tablets of stone that will govern our ethical behavior for all time.

10. Prayer cannot be a request made to a theistic deity to act in human history in a particular way.

11. The hope for life after death must be separated forever from the behavior control mentality of reward and punishment. The Church must abandon, therefore, its reliance on guilt as a motivator of behavior.

12. All human beings bear God's image and must be respected for what each person is. Therefore, no external description of one's being, whether based on race, ethnicity, gender or sexual orientation, can properly be used as the basis for either rejection or discrimination.[10]

The Two Visions Within

The liberal vision, sometimes called "catholic modernism" soon became ensconced in the Episcopal seminaries, where, for the following decades, clergy were formed and indoctrinated. Upon graduation, these same clergy then were placed into ministry positions in the local congregations and dioceses, where the liberal vision was then presented as the gospel. By the turn of the century, 2000, Western Anglican-Ism had become for the most part synonymous with this liberal vision. This is especially true of the Episcopal Church, but also many of the Western provinces in general—i.e., England, Ireland, Canada, etc.

While the liberal vision was gaining ground in the West, the conservative orthodox vision, planted by missionaries in previous eras in Africa,

---

10. *Wikipedia*, s.v. "John Shelby Spong" (section Twelve Points), http://en.wikipedia.org/wiki/John_Shelby_Spong#Twelve_points.

Asia, and South America had grown up into a vibrant new force in the Anglican Communion. The Global South had come of age. The orthodox vision maintained a conservative position on "the faith once delivered to the saints." This phrase contains the understanding that Holy Scripture and the traditional interpretation thereof form the bedrock of doctrine and practice for the church; promotes the acceptance of a plain reading of Scripture as authoritative; and upholds a biblical worldview unfiltered and unmodified by the modern or postmodern paradigms.

The two visions, liberal and orthodox, flow from two competing worldviews, postmodern and biblical. The postmodern worldview presents a closed system of the universe. This view maintains all that exists, either natural or spiritual, is contained in and part of the system. There is no objective reality, or God, that stands above or apart. Creation and creator are one, and our own experience as conscious human beings is what determines what is true. The biblical worldview declares creation and creator distinct from one another. The physical universe exists and is contingent upon the spiritual realm that transcends it. God is objective, above and beyond, and he alone is the final arbiter of what is true. Our part as human beings is to receive his word and come to know him on a journey through this world and on into eternity.

It is interesting to consider the difference between these competing streams of theological expression. Coming down through the modern era and into Postmodernity, the liberal vision has remained lively. That is to say the liberal worldview has continued to develop and morph toward maturity, seeking to engage and draw into itself the populace, the world, and the culture. In short, it is actively engaged in persuasion, and continually producing the next representative. Can the same be said for orthodoxy? Certainly, this is a question worth pondering as we move ahead.

By and large those who hold to the biblical orthodox beliefs have remained faithful and true, even if struggling somewhat to develop relevancy to the surrounding culture. Those who hold to the liberal beliefs have embraced a state of flux —changing, adapting, and revising to the culture so as to be spiritual in the world. These two different systems of beliefs now vie for the heart of Christianity, each providing a radically different answer to the question, "What does it mean to be a Christian?" Within the Anglican Communion we see them both on display and in conflict with one another.

I have heard it said that the United States and England are two nations separated by a common language. For, even though both share a common heritage from the past, today the words and the meanings are set in the context of different cultures, different histories, and a matrix of knowing and perceiving the world that is peculiar to each country. The language sounds the same, but much of what is said means something completely different.

The same holds true for liberal and conservative Anglicans. We are two churches separated by a common language. Although we share a common heritage, the priorities and practice of our faith are set in the context of different theologies, alternative views of the surrounding culture, and a matrix of knowing and perceiving God and the world that is peculiar to each.

Much of what is said in conversation with each other sounds the same, but the meanings are substantially different. Each community may be able to hear the words of the other, but in the end both walk away perplexed not understanding what the other really meant. Perplexity turns to confusion, confusion to frustration, and frustration to anger. We get angry because the others just don't seem to get it. We seem to say the same thing, but then act in ways that are radically different.

Of course, the situation is not as simple as this. A whole spectrum exists in between the extreme left and the extreme right. Individuals, parishes, and dioceses consist of different mixes and opinions. This postmodern tendency to customize our own religious beliefs adds to the complexity and the confusion. Nevertheless, in the final analysis there remain two distinct theological systems, two religious expressions, which are distinct and irreconcilable.

At present both remain conjoined, two churches separated by a common language, the language of Anglican Christianity. Both uphold the Book of Common Prayer as the standard of worship. Both ascribe to tradition, reason, and Scripture as the Anglican way. Both claim to be legitimate heirs of the Anglican tradition. Indeed, both may be justified in doing so, as the Anglican stream has provided a place of nurture for each.

Both theological expressions purport to uphold the truth of the gospel. Both affirm the authority of Holy Scripture. Both hold up Jesus Christ as Savior. Both even maintain that they are orthodox. Like the surface of a lake on a still afternoon, each reflects the surrounding landscape of the Anglican-Ism, in an illusion of unity. But, beneath the surface there is a great divide.

In order to plunge into the depths and see clearly the division that resides there, one must ask questions that break through the surface mirage, questions that are penetrating. For example, we may ask, "Is Jesus Christ the Savior?" All will answer, "Yes." But if we ask, "Who is Jesus?," "What do we mean by the Christ?" or, "What is the nature of sin and salvation?," very different answers will begin to emerge. These answers form the theological presuppositions, which in turn order the faith and practice of each respective church community.

Who is Jesus? What is the gospel? How does Holy Scripture have authority? What is sin? Morality? Is God independent from the universe, or interdependent with it? Is God a personal transcendent being, or a divine immanent force? These questions penetrate the idyllic surface of statements which all claim to adhere to. Beneath the surface we are faced with answers from two separate and distinct theological systems. These systems may be cohesive, in and of themselves, but are radically different from one another.

Once the surface is broken, like a scuba diver we begin to see clearly what lies beneath. Two distinct visions of what it means to be an Anglican, indeed even what it means to be a Christian, have emerged, and there is a great divide between them. This divide will not be breached by simply talking it over in the common language of the surface. Such conversation is merely representative, it simply does not convey the meanings that reside in the depth. The only way this division can be overcome, would be if one or the other abandons their theological presuppositions.

Will this happen? Will liberal Anglicans abandon their commitment to promoting Gay, Lesbian, Bisexual, Transgender inclusiveness, a peace and justice gospel, and the acceptance of all faiths as equivalent paths to God? Will conservative Anglicans abandon their commitment to morality based on an objective scriptural standard, Jesus as the exclusive means of salvation, and a gospel that proclaims the need to convert others to Christianity?

Simply answered, *no*!

Neither liberals nor conservatives will abandon the foundations of their faith as they see it. Whole lives and whole communities of faith are formed and committed to these two increasingly distinct and separate systems of belief. For either of them to cast aside these foundations would be to abandon their understanding of God, and, along with it, the community that is formed around that understanding.

And so we remain divided, two churches, two theologies, separated by a common language. The division will only become greater as time goes on. Unless we honestly acknowledge the divide and embrace a realistic solution, lack of understanding, frustration, and anger will continue to escalate. Eventually, the Anglican Communion will disintegrate as a worldwide body.

The only way to resolve the conflict is through reformation. In order to maintain integrity and fulfill their respective visions, liberals and conservatives must each reform into their own distinctive communities of faith. Attempting to force one side to capitulate to the other will only result in the shredding of all. Through its current actions, the Episcopal Church USA seems to have recognized this, and is actively seeking to grab as much as possible before the breakup gets under way. Conservatives also have followed suit, gathering multiple jurisdictions together to form the new province of the Anglican Church in North America. Yet, I am arguing that the time for waiting is long past. We who are participants in the orthodox vision need to initiate action before it is too late.

The Conservative Vision Intact

The liberal vision for all practical purposes has taken control over the Western provinces and begun the process of bringing everyone into the fold. Conservatives in the Episcopal Church USA began fighting a rearguard action based upon reassertion on the one hand and an exit strategy on the other. Meanwhile, the conservative vision remains intact and vibrant within the Anglican Communion as a whole, due to the commitment and faith of the members in the Global South, especially the churches in Africa.

As the struggle between the two visions continues, their solidarity with conservatives in the West was certified at GAFCON—the Global Anglican Future Conference which took place in Jerusalem 2008. The result of GAFCON was the publication of the Jerusalem Declaration of Orthodox Anglican Faith. This statement that follows offers a prime example of the reassertion of the conservative vision of Christianity within the Anglican-Ism.

The Jerusalem Declaration

In the name of God the Father, God the Son and God the Holy Spirit:

We, the participants in the Global Anglican Future Conference, have met in the land of Jesus' birth. We express our loyalty as disciples to the King of kings, the Lord Jesus. We joyfully embrace his command to proclaim the reality of his kingdom which he first announced in this land. The gospel of the kingdom is the good news of salvation, liberation and transformation for all. In light of the above, we agree to chart a way forward together that promotes and protects the biblical gospel and mission to the world, solemnly declaring the following tenets of orthodoxy which underpin our Anglican identity.

1. We rejoice in the gospel of God through which we have been saved by grace through faith in Jesus Christ by the power of the Holy Spirit. Because God first loved us, we love him and as believers bring forth fruits of love, ongoing repentance, lively hope and thanksgiving to God in all things.

2. We believe the Holy Scriptures of the Old and New Testaments to be the Word of God written and to contain all things necessary for salvation. The Bible is to be translated, read, preached, taught and obeyed in its plain and canonical sense, respectful of the church's historic and consensual reading.

3. We uphold the four Ecumenical Councils and the three historic Creeds as expressing the rule of faith of the one holy catholic and apostolic Church.

4. We uphold the Thirty-Nine Articles as containing the true doctrine of the Church agreeing with God's Word and as authoritative for Anglicans today.

5. We gladly proclaim and submit to the unique and universal Lordship of Jesus Christ, the Son of God, humanity's only Savior from sin, judgment and hell, who lived the life we could not live and died the death that we deserve. By his atoning death and glorious resurrection, he secured the redemption of all who come to him in repentance and faith.

6. We rejoice in our Anglican sacramental and liturgical heritage as an expression of the gospel, and we uphold the 1662 Book of Common Prayer as a true and authoritative standard of worship and prayer, to be translated and locally adapted for each culture.

7. We recognize that God has called and gifted bishops, priests and deacons in historic succession to equip all the people of God for their ministry in the world. We uphold the classic Anglican Ordinal as an authoritative standard of clerical orders.

8. We acknowledge God's creation of humankind as male and female and the unchangeable standard of Christian marriage between one man and one woman as the proper place for sexual intimacy and the basis of the family. We repent of our failures to maintain this standard and call for a renewed commitment to lifelong fidelity in marriage and abstinence for those who are not married.

9. We gladly accept the Great Commission of the risen Lord to make disciples of all nations, to seek those who do not know Christ and to baptise, teach and bring new believers to maturity.

10. We are mindful of our responsibility to be good stewards of God's creation, to uphold and advocate justice in society, and to seek relief and empowerment of the poor and needy.

11. We are committed to the unity of all those who know and love Christ and to building authentic ecumenical relationships. We recognize the orders and jurisdiction of those Anglicans who uphold orthodox faith and practice, and we encourage them to join us in this declaration.

12. We celebrate the God-given diversity among us which enriches our global fellowship, and we acknowledge freedom in secondary matters. We pledge to work together to seek the mind of Christ on issues that divide us.

13. We reject the authority of those churches and leaders who have denied the orthodox faith in word or deed. We pray for them and call on them to repent and return to the Lord.

14. We rejoice at the prospect of Jesus' coming again in glory, and while we await this final event of history, we praise him for the way he builds up his church through his Spirit by miraculously changing lives.

The Great Divide

In the previous chapter we considered the historical paradigm shifts in the West, especially in relation to the Anglican-Ism. These transformations on the grand scale are typically preceded by an emerging crisis, which gradually develops and begins to assert stain on the accepted norms. Finally, a breaking point is reached, then the shift takes place ushering in the new era. The Anglican Church itself has now reached such a breaking point.

Two Visions

The Anglican Communion is living through a paradigm shift of its own. The crisis within Anglican-Ism has been developing for a long time, and now must be resolved. Yet, the existing instruments of unity are insufficient to deal with the problems that now confront us as a church. They must be modified, enhanced, or changed altogether in order to resolve the crisis and set the Anglican Church in proper alignment. Reformation is needed if we are to be effective in our proclamation of the gospel in the new oneworld era.

In a nutshell, the crisis is a conflict between two competing worldviews: The biblical worldview and the postmodern worldview. Worldviews contain the axis of belief, especially religious beliefs, from the answers they provide to questions regarding the nature of God, the universe, and mankind. Both the biblical and the postmodern worldviews present and promote a vision of faith and practice—a liberal vision and a conservative vision. These visions have both grown up in Anglicanism, and thus can both claim to be legitimate heirs. Yet, they are distinct from one another. Each is radically different in the literal meaning of the word radical—at the root. The two are incompatible and irreconcilable. The crisis being, they both seek to control the whole of the Anglican Church in the twenty-first century. Only one can succeed.

At its heart, the Anglican crisis is a Christian crisis. The problems on display within the Anglican Communion have been likened to a long slow motion train wreck. However, the screeching wheels and crunching metal is not limited to Anglicans. The church universal is facing the same problems and dynamics in our time. The question posed to the church is simply this, "What does it mean to be a Christian?"

Within the Anglican-Ism, the two visions promote two very different answers to the question. This is confusing because both claim to represent Anglican/Christian belief. The confusion is deepened by the fact that both utilize language which is recognizable as distinctly Christian. The two visions cannot be reconciled, and they can no longer be maintained in cozy proximity under the banner of one church body. The liberal vision of the western provinces has supporters who are politically astute, well financed, and deeply committed to fulfilling their agenda. The heresy which they promote, like leaven, could permeate the whole of Anglican-Ism.

The great divide in the Anglican stream of Christianity is upon us. The division, which is already a reality beneath the surface, is becoming visible and tangible to all. Common language does not make the English into Americans, nor Americans into English. Neither will it make liberals into conservative Anglicans, nor conservative Anglicans into liberal ones.

The Anglican Communion is in crisis. The time for denial is over. The day is at hand when all must chose to stand on one side of the divide or the other. Orthodox believers must initiate the Anglican reformation of the twenty-first century, to restore and realign the historic Anglican-Ism, reclaiming a genuine expression of Christian faith for the new paradigm. Let us turn then to a deeper consideration of the crisis, the problems, and the possible solutions.

No one can serve two masters,
for either he will hate the one and love the other,
or he will be devoted to the one and despise the other.

—MATTHEW 6:24

4

Crisis

THE TWO VISIONS OF Christian faith and practice described in the previous chapter represent the active expression of radically different theologies. Two opposing worldviews that are each striving for ascendancy within the same community—namely the church. In such a situation a crisis is inevitable. It is a crisis that we now find ourselves in the midst of today: of beliefs and values; of polity and authority; and of relationship and community.

In some ways this current situation is not unlike the crisis of Arianism, which gripped the early church. At heart what was at stake was the very identity of the Christian community. In answer to the question, "What does it mean to be a Christian?," or of equal import, "Who is Jesus?," Arias promoted a different view of Jesus Christ, one that was more acceptable to the prevailing culture of the time. His view made more sense, seemed more reasonable, and was more affirming to humanity. Jesus was a man just like us. He was a created being. As a result, Arianism was very persuasive. Gradually, this alternative viewpoint began to permeate through the greater community of faith. The Roman Empire was on the way to becoming Arian. Missionaries were even sent to the Balkans bearing this gospel message.

However, the opposing worldview of Trinitarian faith, represented by Athanasius, could not yield, mold, nor adapt to the new ideal. It was impossible. Not because of sheer stubbornness, but because of genuine commitment to the veracity of Scripture. Pressure mounted against Athanasius to compromise for the sake of the unity of the church. He was told, "The world is against you," to which he replied, "Then I am against the world." Hence we have the famous quotation, "Athanasius contra mundum!" It is the truth that must be upheld.

This crisis culminated in the Council of Nicaea in AD 325. There Athanasius, and those others with him, prevailed, and the foundation of Christian belief was set on the solid rock of the authority of Holy Scripture, and formulated into a creed of confession. The church continues to declare the Nicene Creed as the cornerstone of our belief to this day.

Like Arianism, the liberal worldview today, with its revised understandings of God and humanity, has slowly and steadily permeated the church in the West. This expression seeks to befriend the surrounding culture, and draw insights from a plurality of sources. This makes more sense to the world we live in, seems more reasonable, more affirming to our mutual humanity. Yet, at heart it promotes a radical change of identity to all who call themselves Christian. What does it mean to be a Christian? Who is Jesus? A very different set of answers are being offered.

As an Anglican priest and rector of St. Luke's Anglican Church, I have experienced firsthand the unfolding of the liberal-conservative schism being played out between the Episcopal Church (TEC) and their Anglican counterparts. At the heart of the matter, there resides a theological divide, which is irreconcilable. It all boils down to two different visions for Christian faith and practice. Each has their own distinct set of core beliefs. Each have their own set of accepted practices. Each provides a definition of what it means to be a Christian, especially in our time.

Let me offer a brief comparative analysis based upon facts, which are easily verifiable.

The Liberal Episcopal Church teaches and promotes:

- Many Ways: all major religions provide equal access to God. Jesus is only the prominent way of Western culture.

- Authority of Spiritual Experience: the subjective understanding of each person is the basis for deciding what is true and/or morally acceptable. The Bible may provide good examples, but does not have objective authority for all generations.

- A Revised Understanding of God, Jesus Christ, and Human Nature: God is a divine spirit found within the physical universe; Jesus Christ is a man that fully accessed this divine spirit in conscious human form, and thus is our prime example; Human Nature is inherently good. Since we are made in God's image, the divine spirit resides in every person. We are all part of God.
- Human Sexuality: affirmed in all the various expressions, according to one's own personal self-identity.

To be clear, I am not suggesting that every member of the Episcopal Church wholly ascribes to the beliefs listed above. But their church as a body has embraced this new form of revised Christianity, it is taught in their seminaries, and their bishops are actively promoting it. Look up the following examples online: Bishop Swing's United Religions Initiative; Presiding Bishop Schori's Prayer to Mother Jesus; Bishop Gene Robinson's Affirmation of LGBT Lifestyle; Bishop Jon Bruno, Apology to Hindus for Christian Mission.

In contrast Anglicans join with Catholics, Orthodox, Evangelicals, and others in maintaining the original Christian beliefs taught by the apostles.

Conservative Anglicans teach and promote:

- One Way: through Jesus alone we are restored in our relationship with God and with one another. He is the fulfillment of all religions.
- Authority of Holy Scripture: The basis of deciding what is true and morally acceptable is given to us in the objective authority of God's word. This remains true for all generations.
- A Traditional Understanding of God, Jesus Christ, and Human Nature: God is the creator of the universe and remains distinct from it; Jesus is both human and divine, the one and only Son of God whose death and resurrection brings us new life. Human Nature is inherently sinful. God's image remains, but it is broken by our willful rejection of his ways.
- Human Sexuality: Affirmed exclusively in marriage between one man and one woman. All other sexual expressions and practices are outside the boundaries set by God.

It is not enough to claim, "We say the Nicene Creed every Sunday," as evidence of Christian belief. One must ask the deeper question, "What exactly do you mean by the words you are reciting?" Liberals have embraced the postmodern spirit of the age in an attempt to be relevant to the culture.

In doing so, they have changed the core beliefs of Christian faith at the very roots. This revision then becomes a pseudo Christianity, which is radically opposed to the original. The two cannot be reconciled by simply saying, "Let's all be friends." We no longer worship the same God.

Those who remain committed to the orthodox worldview cannot change, adapt, nor yield to this new religious movement. It is impossible. Since we are both vying for the same thing, the identity of the church, the crisis has come.

It has been a slowly developing crisis, which began almost unnoticed. The conflict, or set of conflicts, has grown steadily through the end of the twentieth century, and now continues into the twenty-first. The underlying causes finally came to a head within the Anglican Church in 2003 with the election, and subsequent consecration, of Vicky Gene Robinson as bishop of New Hampshire in the Episcopal Church. The first openly practicing homosexual appointed to be a bishop in the church.

Let us take a moment to consider this crisis, the conflicts that brought us here, and the stages and strategies engaged in as a result. In my view there are four distinct possibilities of response to the situation. Some responses which come naturally, and some which require more effort, determination, and clarity of thinking to bring about. The four are:

1. Denial
2. Reconciliation
3. Détente
4. Reformation

Denial

Grandpa used to say, "There has never been a problem I couldn't solve without a healthy dose of pure denial." Grandpa was wrong. Just ask Grandma. Denial does not solve problems, it does not resolve conflicts and it does not take us out of crisis. In fact, it only makes matters worse, prolonging the inevitable. Yet, denial often remains as a preeminent response to difficulties that we find ourselves in, especially difficulties in relationships with one another. Why? Perhaps because it seems easier, and indeed be so in the short run. Perhaps because we don't like confrontation, it makes us uncomfortable. In the life of the church, time progresses slowly. Church time is slow time, so we are not pressed to find a resolution quickly or do the hard work of honesty. Genuine honesty is the opposite of denial.

Denial is an immediate human reaction, and it has been on display as the preeminent strategy throughout the current Anglican crisis. In the early stages when liberal pseudo-Christian doctrine began to permeate the seminaries and pulpits in the West, conservative response was muted. Certainly there was disagreement and a certain wagging of heads. There was a commitment to pray for those who were off track, but not recognition that the communion itself was being threatened. Many thought that even though there are some fringe teachings in seminaries, and even though there are some bishops like Spong who are out there, this does not affect our worship or our communion together. This does not affect our doctrine. After all, doctrine is set in the Book of Common Prayer, and that has not changed.

Liberals declared the highest principle to be unity, and who can argue against that? Schism is the eighth deadly sin. There are many ways of interpreting Scripture, who can know for certain which is right? Let everyone decide for themselves. Let's all stay together, for that is what is most important. We all say the same creed; therefore, we all believe the same thing. And so, the conflicts simmered, and the crisis grew deeper.

When Gene Robinson was elected as the first openly practicing gay bishop, it was time for a reality check. Orthodox and Global South Anglicans issued a warning against his consecration. "Don't do this or you will tear the fabric of the communion at the deepest level"—a good attempt at genuine honesty. In fact, the fabric was already torn. The foundation was split in two. Underneath the house, there already existed a great chasm. Robinson only opened a portal to make it visible.

Denial continued. On the right: this gay bishop thing is an anomaly; it won't happen again. After all it only affects one diocese, New Hampshire. TEC will listen, heed the warnings, and see the error of their ways. This crisis will not get progressively worse. And, on the left: we are sorry you are hurt by our actions. There will be a moratorium on further consecrations like this one. After all, we continue to affirm the 1998 Dar es Salaam accords which affirmed biblical sexual morality as the agreed upon standard for the communion. From both sides it would seem that there is no acknowledgement of the common use of language with inherently different meanings. "Why do we say the same things, but it does not solve the crisis?"

The strategy from the liberal side has been to buy time to allow further permeation of their revised doctrines, by continuing to deny the problem even exists. "Why can't we be friends?" Their trump card is unity, which they use to propel the crisis down through time to give space for pseudo-Christianity to take over.

The strategy from the orthodox side has been to engage in talking. Let's talk it out. Once the liberals understand what they are doing, and how it is affecting our common life, then they will repent. They will change their actions when we talk to them, and declare our position. Let us take a stand for truth, and truth will prevail. We can persuade TEC to repent. The trump card for the orthodox is truth, which they use to try to lever the wayward back into the fold.

The highest principle of unity comes into conflict with the highest principle of truth. Which position has been the most effective so far?

At its heart the crisis is a crisis of authority—spiritual authority. In particular, the authority of Holy Scripture and, more specifically, what do we mean by that phrase. As discussed in the last chapter, both liberals and conservatives invoke the authority of Scripture, using the same language but meaning something completely different. The way in which liberals and conservatives understand the inspiration and authority of Scripture, what each means when they use the terms, and how it applies to the practice of faith makes all the difference.

Inspiration and Authority

When we consider the doctrine of inspiration and authority in Scripture, two dynamics are at work: the human and the Divine. Depending upon the emphasis given to one or the other our understanding of inspiration will be radically altered. In turn this will have direct bearing upon that which we consider to be authoritative in Scripture. Inspiration may be thought of in several differing modes. It may be absolutely divine with the human authors in a sense possessed during the writing. In contrast, it may be dismissed altogether by proclaiming mere human authorship. Inspiration has also been thought of in terms of the person who is reading, rather than the writers of the Holy Scripture. In the postmodern paradigm meaning is not found in the text itself, meaning resides in the reader who imports it into the words being read.

When the divine quality of Scripture is elevated, the authority of Scripture becomes supreme. If every word found in the Bible comes directly from God then there can be no argument. From a conservative perspective this initially seems to be a comfort. We want to affirm that the Bible is God's Word and thereby true and trustworthy. However, when reflecting upon the literal content of Scripture we will soon become uncomfortable. A strictly divine viewpoint gives no room for human, or cultural, elements. We must therefore affirm that women must wear head coverings and keep silent in the church, adulterers are to be stoned, and we should drink a little wine for stomach problems.

On the other hand, when we elevate the human element, then the Bible simply becomes another good book—a Western classic, well worth reading because of the portrayal of Western morality and civilization, but certainly no more authoritative than we would decide to allow it to be. The Bible becomes a record of human experiences and stories depicting human ideas. As such it may be helpful to us in understanding our own experience, but what has authority is the experience itself. This is a good summary of the liberal point of view.

Conservatives maintain that the authority that resides in Scripture is based upon the divine truth inherently contained within it. As we read the Scriptures, the Spirit of God brings that truth to bear upon our desires and our ways of thinking. Thus the power of the Word is a convincing, or convicting, power which cuts through our excuses and deceptions and calls us to be realigned with the truth. "For the word of God is alive and active. Sharper than any double-edged sword, it penetrates even to dividing soul and spirit, joints and marrow; it judges the thoughts and attitudes of the heart" (Heb 4:12). The love and goodness of God represented by the Scripture contains the power to overcome evil and transform the life of individuals and societies. As such, this power stands in direct contradiction with worldly or demonic power which utilizes fear and destruction in a self-serving fashion.

Liberals hold that Scripture is a wonderful record of how men and women experienced the Divine. The stories and thoughts that are represented therein are not necessarily true in the sense that they actually took place, or that they are inherently applicable to all generations. Rather the Scriptures show us the way toward understanding our own experience, as examples and guides. In this manner they have authority, but it is subjective authority relative to the time and culture in which we live.

Authority always operates within the context of community. It is a social phenomenon. It is a paradox of modernity to speak of the authority of the individual. If, as individuals, we reside outside the life of a community our authority is meaningless. It is only when we find our identity as a part of the greater whole that authority then becomes valid. The conservative community of the church proclaims that truth is present in revelation and in Scripture through the original inspiration, therefore these become authoritative. The liberal community of the church proclaims that truth is present in the immediate experience of men and women and the progressive revelation of the Spirit, therefore these become authoritative.

The interrelationships of revelation, inspiration, illumination and authority are complex. When changes occur in our understanding of the nature of one the others are also affected. Ultimately, God is the author of them all, and it is the Word of God which is the underlying essence within each. This sacramental understanding of Scripture provides for us a foundation as we move toward the more difficult task of Christian unity.

The crisis fomented between the liberal and conservative visions is exacerbated by the division over the basic tenets of biblical interpretation. Each has a fundamentally different understanding of what the Bible is, and how it is to be applied to the community of the church. Such misunderstanding can hardly even begin to provide the means for a conversation on the matter, much less be a starting point for the two sides to find agreement and reconciliation. Conservatives and liberals have each set a chief cornerstone of authority upon which their respective communities are built, and the two are in opposition to one another.

Reconciliation

As the Anglican Communion wrestles with the two visions within the proponents of each have set in motion their own particular solution to the conflict. From the liberal camp comes a plea for reconciliation, while conservatives have asserted the need for an Anglican covenant. As solutions to the Anglican crisis, both are woefully inadequate, and in fact have no chance of success. Each offers a false hope, which only serves to propel the conflict further into the future. Such a time delay works to the advantage of the liberal vision, but against those who desire a renewal of the traditional Christian faith.

Reconciliation is hard to argue with. As Christians, we believe that Jesus Christ has reconciled us to God, and given to us the ministry of reconciliation. That is to say that the church is to be God's agent on earth—bearing the good news of his wonderful offer to all the world. This is reconciliation set in a biblical context, describing a restored relationship between God and mankind.

The principles of reconciliation may also be applied in other less theological contexts as well: husbands and wives may be reconciled to each other following marital strife; countries may reconcile their differences prior to warfare; even bank statements need to be reconciled and restored to proper order. Thus, in principle reconciliation removes obstacles, restores relationship, and puts things back into proper order. Therefore, the promotion of reconciliation by TEC as a solution to the Anglican dilemma sounds at first to be the reasonable, and indeed, Christian approach. However, to see clearly we must understand and examine the context to which reconciliation is being applied.

As mentioned, there are many situations theological, personal, and practical where reconciliation is appropriate, but there are also times when reconciliation is impossible, and absolutely wrong: an abused wife must not reconcile with a violent husband, good cannot be reconciled with evil; peace with war; fraud and embezzlement with honesty and integrity. There exist moral absolutes which must not be surrendered for the sake of that which opposes them, or reconciliation becomes compromise.

Returning to the theological context, heresy cannot be reconciled with truth. Yet, this is precisely what the liberals and TEC are seeking to accomplish.

Throughout Holy Scripture reconciliation with God is set in contradistinction with reconciliation with the world: "no one can serve two masters,"[1] "what fellowship has light with darkness,"[2] "you shall have no other gods before me."[3] The reconciliation promoted by TEC is a false solution, precisely because the principle is being applied to a situation regarding truth and heresy. Invoking the principle of the Via Media, this approach attempts to resolve the conflict by mediating a compromise. Yet, God has never allowed for such a compromise when it comes to following him, especially regarding his person, his plan, or his people. In short, God does not compromise with sin.

When seen in this light, the solution of reconciliation waged by TEC becomes nothing less than a strategy utilized for the accomplishment of their own agenda—the victory of the liberal vision. After all, who can argue

1. Matthew 6:24.
2. 2 Cor 6:14.
3. Exod 20:3.

with reconciliation? It sounds so biblical, so loving and true. Therefore, the very use of the word causes Christians to engage with the process, and they are sucked in to a never ending dialogue bent on compromise and capitulation. "We must continue to dialogue until we understand one another and can be reconciled." In other words, until conservatives compromise and accept the liberal vision as the status quo. Buyer beware! Genuine reconciliation is not possible in this context, no matter how appealing it looks, or is made to sound, because God's truth is lost. Scriptural reconciliation with God always requires repentance and obedience to his ways, not the sinful promotion of the self and the ways of man in the name of religion.

While the liberal strategy of reconciliation seeks to use a biblical principle to force a compromise of truth, conservatives have put forth their own solution to safeguard it known as the Anglican Covenant. Frustrated by years of complicity and innuendo on the part of the liberal provinces, Global South Anglicans felt the need for a definitive statement of belief, which all who purport to be Anglican must subscribe to. The Anglican Covenant is in concept a confession of the faith once delivered to the saints—a statement of the core beliefs of the Anglican Church. It is believed that once a covenant is established, order will be restored to the communion. Provinces will self select as to who remains and who departs, because all will be required to ascribe to the covenant in order to be considered part of the Anglican Communion. In a sense we will all be reconciled as a communion by affirming the covenant together.

As many have pointed out, one of the primary reasons for the current crisis is that there is presently no central authority within the collection of provinces of the worldwide Anglican Church. Each is autonomous unto itself. There is no pope, no council of bishops, nor a committee that can make a judicial ruling regarding either faith or practice, as applicable to the whole. Rather than establish such authority, the Anglican Covenant extends a long process of statements, reports, communiqués, and conferences that have done nothing to address the real issue—namely, a new heretical movement which seeks to supplant the Christian faith in Anglican-Ism. As discussed previously, this crisis is a conflict between two competing worldviews: postmodern and biblical.

Therefore, as a solution to the crisis of Anglican-Ism, the Anglican Covenant is dead on arrival. It is doomed to the same fate that claimed the effectiveness of its predecessors, including Lambeth '98, the Windsor Report, Dar es Salaam, and even Holy Scripture itself. All have been taken down and tied in knots by the relativism that operates as a core principle of the liberal vision. Subjective interpretation rules out any possibility for agreement upon a written doctrinal covenant. Even if such a document was written with amazing clarity and unparalleled acumen, multiple and vagrant interpretations will be pried, cajoled, and twisted forth from the subjective understanding of those who are invested in making the covenant serve their own agenda. Remember, meaning is not found in the words of the text, the reader imports their own meaning into it. This is standard operation within the liberal theology of TEC, subjective interpretation has authority in matters regarding faith and practice, and especially regarding anything that is written. In the end the Anglican Covenant will be meaningless, because any and every possible meaning will be derived from it, and attached to it by the liberals.

That said, I must add that the covenant holds some promise as a foundation for a new Anglican Fellowship. Before casting the covenant out altogether, it is necessary to state the great benefit that it does make available, especially for the purposes of reformation for the orthodox Anglican churches. The beauty and strength of the covenant resides in the clarity which it brings in expressing the biblical worldview. The covenant is foundational as a means of binding together like minded orthodox Anglicans worldwide. It provides the confession of faith vital for genuine unity based in truth. However, as we shall discuss, the covenantal statement is not able to accomplish the task alone. What is also required are clear boundaries, central authority, and a certified method of interpretation.

Détente

The stages we are discussing in regards to the crisis that has now fomented in the Anglican communion is not unlike the process that many marriages go through in seeking to work through the difficulties in an intimate relationship. First denial, the problems do not exist, or they will go away if we just ignore them. When that does not work, counseling is the next step. This is the attempt at reconciliation of difficulties through mediation. As a priest, this is often the stage when a couple arrives in my office. Typically the crisis is upon them in the form of one or the other stating, "I want a divorce!" Various principles can be taught, and exercises assigned in an attempt to break through the stone walls, sometime with success—other times not.

When denial has been in vain, and reconciliation fruitless, the next stage in managing the crisis becomes détente. The decision is made, either consciously or unconsciously, to just tough it out. The idea is that this is a good as it gets. Things are not going to change, and besides it is just taking too much energy to try to work things out. Energy that could be expended on other parts of life which each of the parties value—whether or not the other values them as well no longer matters.

Détente is a kind of truce. You live your way and I will live my way, and we agree not to harass one another, or try to change one another to our point of view. We have tried to do so and it did not work, and it has proven to be not worth the fight. Instead, we will continue in our association together, because that is important.

We will never agree on the truth, but must maintain unity, or at least the appearance of unity, for that appearance gives us an assurance of stability. Also, that appearance maintains our sense of respectability to the world around us. Of course, all of this is merely a facade covering the irreconcilable differences beneath.

Détente is not all that different from denial. Both leave the main issues and the underlying causes of those issues intact. It comes from a lack of will to take action. At this stage of the crisis, the contestants pull back into their respective corners, like boxers who have grown weary through the rounds of a heavyweight fighting match. They seek solace and strength from their supporters—a chance to breathe and apply salve to the wounds. As the fight continues to wait in the ring, they become reluctant to step back in for further punishment, and may simply begin to dance around each other rather than continue the fight.

The above analogy is especially fitting when we observe the state of the whole Anglican Communion at this time. Since the crisis began, we have been through round after round of effort in seeking to overcome the opposition. This has brought us to a time of détente. Liberals have drawn up into their corners, which by the way occupy most of the main offices within the structure of the existing Anglican Communion. Their strategy is to marginalize the orthodox, and paralyze further attempts to effect change. Not to be undone, conservatives/orthodox have moved to create their own alternative structures of the Global Anglican Fellowship. Nevertheless, all remain as participates in the Anglican Communion as a whole. Certainly, not all consider themselves in communion with one another, but nevertheless all remain in association. It is regularly reported by the world at large, "There is no schism in the Anglican Communion." This means we are viewed as being together as one, and the appearance of respectability is maintained. The facade remains intact.

This stage of détente can be clearly evidenced in the functions and events of the communion at large, as well as in the actions of the recognized leaders and "instruments of unity." Take for example the last Lambeth conference, an event that occurs every ten years, and draws together the bishops and archbishops of the entire communion for a meeting of minds and faith at Lambeth Palace in England. In the months prior to the last event in 2008, the Archbishop of Canterbury, Rowan Williams, consistently took the position in his statements and writings that all simply needed to live together. That is to say, don't try to fix the problem, because it just takes too much energy. Indeed, Williams' essays are so dense as to form a kind of détente in and of themselves.

When the conference was finally convened, the respective combatants arrived with their own corners already staked out. Each brought with them a team of support, and joined with the others of like mind. The theme of the conference, as set by liberals who control the agenda, was Indaba—*indaba* being an African word which signifies the action of talking to one another. The idea and practice of indaba is that those who do not know each other, those who have different points of view, even those who are in conflict with each other, can simply gather together to talk and listen. Thereby understand each other. The bishops came, they indaba-ed together, and they understood nothing was changed and nothing was going to change. Following the conference the crisis continued as before, in the stage of détente. I would argue that this is the stage we continue in to this day—indaba forever.

To be fair to the principle of détente, a time of pulling back from active conflict can at times be beneficial in moving toward a resolution of the crisis. As long as pulling back doesn't turn into sitting down. A time of truce can often give place for the hard work needed to move combatants from the ring to back outside the arena, where they can go on living their lives. Sometimes détente gives a chance for diplomacy to work, and mutually agreed upon solutions to be put into effect. In certain situations, or circumstances, this can be the case. But, is this something that can take place in Anglicanism or Christianity as a whole? Can détente provide a way forward when we are dealing with a crisis that envelopes the very heart and soul of Christian faith? As discussed in the last chapter the answer is simply, *no*!

Reformation

Denial, reconciliation, and détente are all merely stopgap measures that propel the crisis onward down through time. They are not bringing resolution. The healthy solution is the proper setting of boundaries, and the enforcement of discipline. Only this will undo the false dichotomy between unity and truth, and set the Anglican Communion back on the right foundation. Unity based on adherence to truth. The apostolic truth found in the Holy Scripture. Rather than the incessant talking of Indaba, we need to take action. We need reformation.

Reformation is often thought of as synonymous with schism. Certainly the Protestant Reformation resulted in the splintering of the church into many different groups. But, this does not necessarily need to be the case. The pressing need to restore our common life back to its biblical roots, calls for us to re-form our fellowships in such a way that we gather the fragments back together in a cohesive whole. The process is not unlike the remodeling of a house. The foundation must first be shored up and leveled where needed. Some walls are chosen to remain, some are torn down. New doors and windows may be added, while old ones that have openings no longer desired are closed up. In the end, a home emerges that now fulfills the purposes needed and releases the energy of the family who lives there. The Anglican-Ism needs a new house to dwell in. It is up to us to build it.

The problems that underlie the crisis of Anglicanism are often overlooked in a passionate debate about the symptoms. Solutions proposed and discussed along the way come from within the dysfunctional system itself. The attempt to unravel the mess while utilizing the same processes, assumptions, polity, and methods that created the crisis to begin with is doomed to fail. Failure from my point of view means the liberal postmodern worldview will eventually take over.

The problem is not the "gay issue." The problem is the theological grid—first principles, presuppositions, and premises—that allow the gay issue to be an issue in the first place. At heart is a theology of monism which is the belief or understanding that God and the universe are one. Rather than a classic Christian belief in a transcendent God who created the universe yet is separate and distinct from it. In the monistic worldview God and universe are interconnected and interdependent upon one another. God is changing and evolving and the universe is changing and evolving. God is dependent upon and contained within the physical order; the physical order is dependent upon and contained within God. The older theological term for this is pantheism—meaning God is within the world; the newer more sophisticated expression is panentheism—meaning the world is within God. It is important to note that this is the view held by many Eastern religions, like the Hindus, who understand a divine spiritual reality that undergirds all of the physical reality with which we interact.

Monism is one of the basic tenets of the postmodern paradigm, and lays the foundation for the principles of pluralism and tolerance that follow. The acceptance of monism as the chief corner stone of a theological grid allows for the promotion of all religions as equal paths to God. They are like independent oil wells of the spiritual life that drill down to tap into the divine reservoir waiting underneath all. In a sense this is very much the viewpoint of the liberal "Christian" thinkers of modernity. Paul Tillich, remember, describes God as "the Ground of all Being," teaching a radicalized immanence that is essentially the same as monism. This worldview leads to radically different conclusions to the basic questions of; who or what is God? Who is Jesus? What is the nature of humanity? Sin? Salvation? Church? Spirit? and so on. If God, the divine reality is within all things, including human beings, how then can a loving sexual relationship between two men, or between two women be constituted as sinful, or morally wrong. Or for that matter between a man and several wives in polygamy, or two couples joining in intimacy with each other in polyamory. The Christian church would be wrong to quickly dismiss this theological grid as irrelevant or nonthreatening, for it continues to be proven very influential in our time, and is quickly becoming the foundation for the emerging oneworld religion.

The historic opportunity for reformation and revival is slowly passing by. Rather than denial, attempts at reconciliation, and/or détente, what is needed is action. Action taken in the formation of an Anglican Council, one given the mandate to discern truth from error, good from evil, and one that has the authority to act accordingly. Historically this is exactly what the church did at the Council of Nicaea. What then is the process, specifically, for the Anglican Communion to act with the same vigor and results as the early church acted? The discussion above has been more or less theoretical. Let us move on to a consideration of the actions and events required to effect such a reaffirmation of Christian faith in the Anglican expression in which we participate—noting from the onset that such a reaffirmation will in fact result also in a reformation of the Anglican-Ism as well. Thus, as we turn toward the next chapter, "Anglican Manifesto," we are

Anglican Manifesto

in actuality beginning a discussion of the need and process for reformation within the Anglican Church, and extending beyond from there to worldwide Christianity.

I am like a man throwing matches at a haystack,
Hoping that it will light a blaze.

—FR. JACK ESTES

5

Anglican Manifesto

SINCE THE TIME OF the Reformation, the Anglican Church has nestled comfortably between the shores of the Catholic and Protestant expressions of Christian belief. The famous "Via Media" of Anglican-Ism, the middle way, beckons to those who find satisfaction in its appeal to a comprehensive approach to Christian faith and practice. The Anglican Church has maintained a balanced tradition which holds onto the essentials, while allowing for a grace filled approach to much of religious life which is considered peripheral, or at least preferential.

For centuries this middle way has held true. The genius of Anglican-Ism in allowing for differences, while asserting minimalist dogma, has charted a safe course through the religious conflicts of the Enlightenment and Modernity. Anglican comprehensiveness assured a certain liberty from strife, by providing a measured autonomy for the provinces which circumvent the globe. Yet, it is this very comprehensiveness that has given place to an increasingly broad theological spectrum, which is now finding expression within the worldwide communion. The acceptance of all manner of doctrine and practice, combined with the lack of any central adjudicating authority, has brought us to the crisis we are now living through. It is a crisis of competing worldviews: the liberal postmodern worldview vs. the traditional biblical worldview.

As discussed previously, the heresies of our time are monism, pluralism, and relativism, all carefully blended and promoted under the banners of love, tolerance, and social justice. Taken together these form the axis of the liberal worldview, and a foundation for the emerging new oneworld religion. This new religious movement has gained traction in the church, and in many cases has already overtaken it. We should not minimize the subtly of this heresy, nor the promotion of it, because it finds expression through the very language of the creeds of orthodoxy.

In contrast, traditional Christianity is based in a biblical worldview that includes: the exclusive nature of salvation through the person of Jesus Christ; a commitment to the objective authority of the Holy Scripture for all times and all places; and the dualism of God as transcendent creator, wholly separate from the creation itself. These stand in direct spiritual opposition to this new liberal religious endeavor, and, in truth, cannot be reconciled with it.

The question now foisted upon the Anglican Communion is, "How do we cope with this situation?" How can we continue to function with two opposing worldviews competing for control in our midst? The answer, simply put, is we cannot. The impossibility of such a task is easily observed in the events of the past few years. We cannot continue this dance of orthodoxy and heresy. Traditional Anglicans are facing a heretical agenda that is intricate and far deeper beneath the surface than the mere "gay bishop" issue. We are facing a theological conflict that is intractable. Further conversation/

dialogue/indaba/statements/communiqués and proposed ratification of solutions that are somehow representative of both worldviews is futile.

The Anglican Communion is drowning in a sea of words. The solutions being put forth continue the process by offering yet more words. A drowning man is not saved by pouring more water over his head, what is needed is a life raft. The solution is painfully obvious. In order to restore the bonds of Christian community, instead of more carefully crafted words action is required. The Anglican Communion must act to find, or to create, a central authority. Only then will we find ourselves standing once again on solid ground. We must act to establish proper biblical boundaries, which prevent the influx from the spirit of the age that surrounds us.

With boundaries and a central authority in place, we must then continue to have the courage to act and enforce them.

This crisis is a crisis of authority, and cannot be resolved through talking incessantly. The vacant center may have once been a source of Christian largess to an Anglican Church spread at great distances around the world. But, this was long before a new religious movement arose to challenge core Christian beliefs under the guise of Anglican comprehensiveness. The openness that once allowed the gospel to flow out to the culture has now become a liability. The arrows have been reversed bringing in beliefs and practices antithetical to the Christian faith.

The crisis that is upon us is one which requires action. Reformation is needed. Transformation is required. We need changes that will result in a substantially different expression in the life of our church by those who are willing to embrace it: reformation that includes definitive boundaries, a recognized central authority, and which certifies the biblical worldview. The action required is nothing short of formal separation between the competing worldviews and their respective church communities. Naturally, this will bring major changes to the Anglican-Ism, to its polity, to its structures, and to its relationships between member provinces. Some of those relationships will be over; some of those relationships will grow stronger and deeper as we move into the future.

The issue that must be addressed by the Anglican Communion is that of the postmodern worldview growing in its midst, and the corresponding development of a oneworld religion. It is an issue of theological meaning and interpretation, of right doctrine and right practice. It is an issue of Christian identity. As Anglicans, it is not enough to simply restate the Lambeth Quadrilateral as the basis of our common life: the Sufficiency of

Scripture; Office of the Bishop; Creeds; and Sacraments. Each of these is defined and finds expression from the theological foundation beneath the surface. Differing theologies produce different definitions and answers to the inherent questions being raised. What then is needed for clarity? The kind of clarity which also produces unity, for genuine unity does not exist apart from truth —truth which is acknowledged and agreed upon. There is no division between unity and truth found in the Holy Scripture. The community of believers is unified, because they know the truth and are careful to guard the truth.

Using the cornerstones of the Lambeth Quadrilateral, let us consider that which is necessary to produce truth and unity:

1. Scripture contains all things necessary . . .

This is a lovely sentiment which we would all like to believe in. Yet, simply stating this as fact will not ameliorate the friction within the Anglican Communion, nor solve the ongoing frustrations of the various factions. This is because we have not yet taken the time and done the hard work of defining what we mean by "scripture," nor by what we mean by "sufficient." Thus, two radically opposed worldviews, which have radically different meanings for these terms are able to affirm that yes Scripture is sufficient and then go and act out in ways completely at odds with one another. This is because each has a different means of interpretation. In order to resolve this issue, the solution is to take a step further and enact an authoritative method of biblical interpretation—one that is accepted as the standard for all Anglican churches. Only in this manner can we overcome the relativism of the postmodern paradigm, which declares, "You have your interpretation and I have mine." Whatever it may be cannot be challenged, because we each put our own meaning into the text.

As Anglicans we need a clearly defined method of biblical interpretation, which is in fact biblical! Only by agreeing on such, will we reverse the postmodern premise that the person brings the meaning to the text. The Greek term for this is *eisegesis*, which is rooted in pride. By agreement on proper guidelines of interpretation as a standard to be adhered to, we reinforce Christian belief in the eternal and living quality of the Word that speaks the truth of God to all generations. We reaffirm the principle of *exegesis*, which is rooted in humility. Humbly we allow the Word to speak and align our lives to suit what God is saying to us, rather than realigning the Word to suit our lives. A standard for biblical interpretation must include the following principles and presuppositions:

- Meaning and authority are inherent in the Word
- Scripture interprets Scripture
- The whole context of Scripture always considered with each individual passage
- Proper consideration of genre, redaction, metaphor, poetry and prose, etc.
- Theological method based on Christian worldview
- Essential boundaries of what is or is not considered valid

In addition the standard must be subject to the councils of the church, reviewed, explained and taught to all members of the fellowship.

2. Creeds are a sufficient statement of faith . . .

The early church began with a simple confession of faith in Jesus as the Messiah—Jesus Christ is Lord. Soon this became expanded in the expression of the Apostles' Creed, which articulates a more detailed version of the basic tenets of the faith. This was sufficient for a historical season, but over time new challenges emerged. The church was confronted with heretical positions regarding the person of Christ, which began to become infused into the main of Christian belief and practice. To face these challenges the early church initiated a plan of action that resulted in setting things back in proper order. Their approach was as follows:

A. Gathered together in council

B. Discerned truth from error

C. Declared that which was orthodox (right doctrine)

D. Expanded the Creed appropriately

E. Required assent to remain in fellowship

The result of this process was the production of a restatement of Christian belief in clear and succinct terms, one that corrected false doctrines and set boundaries to prevent their reoccurrence. When further Christological or theological controversies came along, the process above was repeated. Thus, for example, the Council of Nicaea expanded the Apostles' Creed to certify Christian truth in the face of Arianism, defining more precisely what was meant by the words describing Jesus as the Son. The Council of Chalcedon further refined the creed in response to the Eutychian controversy, which attempted to redefine the nature of Christ in solely divine terms.

Anglican Manifesto

One need only compare the Apostles' Creed with the Nicene Creed to observe this process in operation. Due to theological/christological revisions which were popular at the time, nevertheless off track, the council of the church recognized the need to expand and clarify exactly what the creed was saying. In particular, they were careful to define exactly who Jesus is in relation to God the Father. "The only begotten" was no longer sufficient. Now a fuller explanation was required: "God from God, light from light, true God from true God, begotten not made, of one being with the Father. Through him all things were made . . ." This expanded definition was necessary because the foremost heresies that confronted the early church were centered around the person and nature of Christ: modalism, docetism, adoptionism, etc.

So once again, let us consider the process from a broader historical viewpoint:

- Faithful church confesses beliefs through creed
- Heretical thought and teaching gains traction
- Heresies threaten to overtake church community
- Council convenes, discerns truth, and brings correction
  - Orthodoxy restated
  - Creed expanded, clarified, and defined
- Heresy purged
- Assent required to remain in fellowship
- Faithful church confesses beliefs through creed

Clearly, we are living through stages two and three in the present moment, as Anglicans, participating in the Anglican Communion, and indeed, as Christians, participating in the worldwide church. Heretical thought and teaching are threatening to overtake the church. Practices which would have been considered anathema for generations of the faithful are subtly being introduced and celebrated, because they are the new accepted norms for the culture around us. Please understand this is not just an Anglican problem. When I say that the church is at risk, I mean the universal church. If you are reading this from the position of being in a different fellowship in the body of Christ, I mean your church. We are living in a new paradigm.

An underlying principle in operation within the matrix of the new heresy comes from the postmodern view of language and meaning in general. Language is merely the touchstone of experience. Meaning, per se, is not found in the words written; meaning is brought to the text by the reader himself. This is, in my opinion, a classic error of eisegesis, imposing ones own meaning into the text, rather than exegesis, extracting the intended meaning from the text. When this heretical principle is applied to standard statements of Christian belief and practice, such as the creeds, the words, or terms, or language, is retained, but the meanings beneath the words are changed. In fact it allows for whatever meaning one may deem fit and proper humanly speaking.

For example:

> God the Father = The Holy, Transcendent, Creator of the Universe
>
> First Person of the Trinity
>
> —*monotheism*
>
> *or,*
>
> The divine creative force found within all things and all people
>
> —*pantheism*
>
> *or,*
>
> The universe as a divine conscious thought that contains all things and people within itself
>
> —*panentheism*
>
> Jesus the Christ = The Incarnate Savior
>
> Second Person of the Trinity
>
> —*monotheism*
>
> *or,*
>
> The apogee of humanity—an enlightened master
>
> The perfect human who fully realized and participated with the divine within
>
> *or/and,*
>
> The one who shows us the way to realize that we are also divine
>
> —*humanism*

> Holy Spirit = Comforter, Counselor, Guide
>
> Third Person of the Trinity
>
> —*monotheism*
>
> or,
>
> The divine evolutionary force which interconnects and motivates the people and events of history all in an ever upward spiral toward consciousness and the goal of divine oneness of all things
>
> —*monism*

If you are thinking, this sounds a lot like Star Wars—"The force be with you"—you are not far off. Star Wars was produced in the 1970s and displays the transition to the postmodern social paradigm. Yet, even Star Wars retains a "dark side of the force," which could be considered sin. Within the definitions of the new postmodern heresy, sin is equated only with ignorance. Sin means that we have not yet gained the knowledge of our participation with the divine within us. Along with the table above, this understanding serves to make the point, that while many can with good conscience confess the same words of the Nicene Creed, each one may be confessing something radically different, and opposed to the meanings assumed there by the Christian church throughout the ages.

3. Bishops are the overseers of the church . . .

In too many ways the office of bishop has become an exercise of politics. Especially in the West, politically minded clergy rise to the top and put into effect the agenda of their constituents. Even among orthodox dioceses, often the bishop is regarded as the chief pastor, a kind of super rector for the people. I advocate a return to the classic understanding of the episcopate. Bishops are the continuation of apostolic ministry, primarily given to be defenders of the faith. They are to be the chief theologians of the church, with pastoral considerations subordinate. As such, bishops set the standards, enforce the boundaries, and are themselves subject to one another in council, so that error and spiritual malaise do not have place to infect the church.

Anglicans must come to agreement on what the office of bishop entails, and who is eligible to hold such office. In addition, the bishop is the visible connection to the larger fellowship. Thus, the question of how, where, and under what guidelines a college of bishops will be convened, or a council of bishops will operate must be determined. This is especially true concerning the discipline of the church by the bishops, and the discipline of bishops by the bishops. These standards need to be clearly articulated. The great gapping hole in the side of a healthy Anglican fellowship is the lack of boundaries and discipline. Anglican comprehensiveness without them does not, and has not, produced Anglican cohesiveness. Conversely Anglican comprehensiveness with boundaries and discipline will equate to Anglican cohesion and health, and would be quite a sight for the world to see.

4. Sacraments convey the grace of God . . .

Sacramental theology has often been a point of contention within the factions of Christianity. One of the strengths of the Anglican-Ism is the willingness to allow for the mystery of God's grace, his presence, and his love to flow through the sacraments of Baptism and Holy Communion, without strict human definition. Much of the crisis we now face requires more stringent definition and clarity. However, the sense of the real presence of God in the sacraments goes beyond this kind of endeavor. Nevertheless, we do need to be clear about who God is, the nature of his grace, and the reasons why we as human beings are in need of it.

Sacraments are the means by which God's immanence is made manifest, but this cannot be divorced from his transcendent qualities or everything in worship becomes unbalanced. In the following chapters, I will argue for an expansion of our understanding of the sacramental nature of creation. The principle that all things are available for God to use in manifesting himself could become a theological foundation from which to build unity across denominational lines. Catholic, evangelical, charismatic, and liberal expressions all focus on particular vibrant qualities within the whole of Christian faith. Each of these qualities, whether word, sacrament, gifts of the Spirit, or service to the poor, are all in fact grounded in a greater sacramental understanding of our relationship with God.

The interrelationship between a biblical worldview and a sacramental worldview will be addressed in the next chapter; nevertheless the concept is one that begins to cement the building blocks of reformation into a sure foundation. The two capital S sacraments, Baptism and Eucharist, form the chief cornerstones, and must continue to take special precedent because of their preeminence in Scripture. In considering the Anglican reformation ahead, such an understanding of sacramental theology may prove to be a key piece in the revival of the whole.

Anglican Manifesto

Throughout this analysis and discussion we have considered the statement of the Lambeth Quadrilateral—the ways in which it has functioned as a statement of faith for the Anglican Church, and the ways in which it is currently found lacking. The crisis now upon us requires that we move beyond assumed meanings, and establish the criteria necessary for certainty in our beliefs. To set the church back on a sure foundation, let us engage in the same process of the early church:

Convene the Council

—recognize/discern the heresies that confront us

Clarify, expand, and define orthodoxy—right belief

—write a clear and succinct statement

Continue as the faithful church in confession

—let us be certain about what we are confessing

Most importantly we must set appropriate theological boundaries, and enforce the boundaries that are set. Assent to right Christian belief is required to remain within Christian fellowship. Those who are inflicted with heresy and cannot let go of it, the church must let go of them. Pray for them, certainly. Persuade them to return, patiently. However, we can ill afford to continue to waste time and energy, or risk remaining in fellowship with them, without risking the soul of the church in the new oneworld paradigm of the twenty-first century.

In truth, we do not have fellowship, in the biblical sense of the word, with those who are caught up in other religions or have put their faith in anyone or anything other than Jesus Christ, as revealed and explained in the Holy Scripture and confessed by the church throughout history. Jesus has commanded us to be compassionate. He did not command us to be tolerant, especially in the way the term is used in the present. Compassion means to suffer along with. Tolerance means to simply leave them to their own devices, however far from God that may take them. As Christians, we are called to speak the truth in love.

As we seek to make the transition from talking to acting, and to develop a plan of action, let us keep in mind some key principles in all we consider:

1. Clear definition for all words, terms and concepts

—*meanings can no longer be assumed they must be explained*

2. Succinct expression of the required components

—*fewer words chosen more carefully will have greater effect for real solutions*

3. Truth and Unity are inseparable

—*needed to maintain a biblical basis for fellowship*

4. Words must be used only as an incentive for action

—*more words describing the problem will not effect a solution*

The result of the Anglican Reformation of the twenty-first century will be a worldwide church community that will no longer be the Anglican Communion as we know it today. A new community that, I will argue, will even need to be called by a new name. New wine must be put in new wineskins, or else the bottles will break. Perhaps, the Anglican Fellowship of the Christian church would be a more appropriate description of who we really are in Christ, or rather who we will become.

The Anglican Reformation of the Twenty-first Century

In order for the traditional Anglican churches, who are committed to the biblical worldview to flourish, or perhaps even survive, we must commit ourselves to the action of reformation. Not only for our sakes, but to prepare for our role in the uniting of the Christian church worldwide, which we are moving toward in the future. In the previous chapters I have expounded these ideas more fully, and laid the foundation for that which I assert here. What follows are the actions, processes, and the requirements needed to effect the reformation and revival of the worldwide Anglican Church:

(1) Acknowledge that Reformation is Needed

Denial is no longer an option, although it is so much easier than actually doing something. Facing the facts, and acknowledging the need are both actions. They are the actions which begin the process of reformation. To begin, we must recognize that the Anglican Communion is completely mired, bogged down, drowning in a sea of words, and that a new and different approach is the only solution.

(2) Gather an Executive Council to Begin the Reformation Process

Ultimately, I am advocating that a new Anglican Fellowship be established and governed on a conciliar based model, the churches/provinces in council with one another deciding right doctrine and right practice. In order to set the stage for a larger council of the Anglican churches, an

Anglican Manifesto

executive council comprised of leaders who are committed to reformation needs to come together, draft the agenda, and set the plan in motion. The selection of such leadership should not be difficult to discern, as the champions of orthodoxy are well known among us.

Tasks:

A. Clarify the Anglican Covenant and include necessary boundaries and enforcement

B. Establish an authoritative method for biblical interpretation

C. Write an expanded definition of the terms and concepts found in the creeds to insure proper theological use, and to certify the truth within

D. Draft a basic statement of belief in the orthodox biblical worldview required for participation in a provincial council, or certify the covenant for this purpose

3. Convene a Provincial Council

The new Anglican Fellowship will come into being when a worldwide council is convened, which represents the provinces, dioceses, parishes, and various jurisdictions who are willing to commit to the traditional biblical worldview. The council is charged with declaring the right doctrine, orthodoxy, and the right practice, orthopraxis, that is acceptable in the Anglican Fellowship of the Christian church. Furthermore, the council must set in place the governing structures and means of relationship between the churches. These structures and relationships must include an accountability to one another that is uncompromising. Autonomy may no more rule the day, for without accountability, boundaries, and a central authority; we may as well stay in the mess we are already in, because that is where we will end up once again.

Tasks:

A. Affirm the commitment and orthodoxy of all who would continue in fellowship

B. Confirm a covenant statement that establishes the biblical worldview and includes necessary boundaries and consequences—Covenant

C. Set in place a proper governance for the new fellowship

D. Establish a central authority representative of the fellowship to adjudicate on issues of faith and practice—a star council of bishops and theologians which address questions and issues as they arise

E. Separate from the Old Structures of the Anglican Communion

Those who wish to move forward in a decidedly orthodox Christian expression of Anglicanism will be welcomed into participation in the new fellowship. Those who have committed to the liberal postmodern worldview must be left to their own devices. Certainly, we can continue to pray for their repentance. We must act toward them charitably, with compassion, but we no longer can continue joined together with them in communion—"what fellowship has light with darkness?"[1] The world will cry schism. Let them. We must go on proclaiming the gospel, as the new oneworld paradigm takes over in place of the postmodern era.

The four steps listed above seem simple, yet each one is dense with the actions needed to facilitate the Anglican Reformation of the twenty-first century. Many of the principle strengths of the Anglican-Ism may be retained as we move from the old vessel to the new, and well they should be. We are not abandoning our heritage, rather we are purifying it. It is the weaknesses of the Anglican-Ism which must be jettisoned: the lack of clear boundaries and a central authority which have lead us into the quagmire; the openness to being directed by the belief systems of the surrounding culture which has drawn us away from our calling as the prophetic community of God; and the reliance on structures and solutions based in paradigms gone by which are no longer effective in the emerging oneworld era.

This Anglican Manifesto is merely an extended essay from which volumes of research and materials may be written. Yet, my purpose in writing in the brief time granted to me is to say to all faithful Anglican Christians, "Now is the time to act." I write from the sincere belief that a whole and complete, vibrant Anglican expression of orthodox Christianity will be poised to bring the gospel to the world of this century. Finally, a reformed, revitalized Anglican Fellowship will stand as a central catalyst to connect and unite Christendom in ways we can only begin to imagine. The following resolution sums up the points above and is submitted for the consideration of all concerned:

The Anglican Reformation of the Twenty-First Century

Resolution

Whereas the openness and comprehensive nature of Anglican-Ism has resulted in the rise of a new religious movement within the Anglican Church,

---

1. 2 Cor 6:14.

Anglican Manifesto

which is based on progressive, postmodern, and monistic theologies that are contrary to the biblical worldview;

Whereas the provinces promoting this liberal vision have been and continue to be a integral component of the Anglican Communion, with members participating at every level of leadership, thus effectively blocking any correction from within;

Whereas the Anglican Communion is hopelessly mired in a conflict between two competing religions, or worldviews, which are incompatible and irreconcilable, resulting in an endless waste of time and energy expounded in an ongoing stream of dialogue, meetings, statements, and procedures;

Whereas within the existing ethos of the Anglican Communion there exists neither the will nor the means to resolve this crisis, whether by reference to the foundational documents and principles which have comprised our common life, nor by the four instruments of unity charged with ordering our common relationships: The Archbishop of Canterbury; Anglican Consultative Council; the Lambeth; or the Provincial Primates; and

Whereas the current crisis poses an ever increasing danger that a worldwide body of Christians who worship together in the Anglican tradition may be lost altogether through disintegration, dissipation, or disillusionment, or even completely overtaken by the postmodern worldview at work within its boundaries; now, therefore, be it

Resolved, that the time of reformation is at hand:

1. The need for reformation of the whole Anglican Communion is acute, and should be immediately acknowledged by all Anglicans formed and committed to a traditional Christian/biblical worldview. Including: archbishops and bishops; priests and deacon; laity, vestries, and conventions;

2. Since the Anglican Reformation of the twenty-first century cannot be effected within the polity and structures of the present Anglican Communion, through existing procedures, statements, nor four instruments of unity, new conciliar structures of polity and oversight must be activated. New wine must be put in new wineskins;

3. Because the existing statements of faith—Holy Scripture, creeds, and Lambeth Quadrilateral—while sufficient in meaning in and of themselves, are now subject to the importation of any and all interpretations and theological methods common to the postmodern era, including

those radically different and heretical to traditional Christian belief. Therefore, the Anglican reformation of the twenty-first century must include clear and authoritative guidelines for biblical interpretation, as well as definitions, and meanings correspondent to all statements of belief. Boundaries to be set and enforced among participating members;

4. A new Anglican Fellowship of the Christian church shall be brought into being, that will be committed to a ordering of common life by means of a conciliar polity. Such fellowship will maintain regular councils of all bishops, and/or with other appointed leaders, to discuss the mind of the church. In keeping with the conciliar model, an additional council consisting of one representative from each province will be appointed to act as a central authority within the Fellowship, adjudicating in matters of faith and practice; and

5. The Anglican Reformation of the twenty-first century will not look to itself as the final end of the process, but will continue to seek out and join with other Christian fellowships who, finding themselves in similar circumstances, have committed to upholding the traditional biblical world view. As we move out of the historical paradigm of postmodernity, and shift into the emerging oneworld era, the new Anglican Fellowship will seek to be a catalyst for the reunification of Christendom in general, in order that Christians everywhere may join together as the Oneworld Church comprised of all faithful to Jesus Christ as Lord, and ready to meet the challenge of the emerging Oneworld Religion.

I call upon our leaders—archbishops and bishops. I call upon our clergy—priests and deacons. I call upon all Christian men and women within the Anglican churches worldwide. Let us discern the time, and complete the task appointed to us. The new Anglican Fellowship of the Christian church awaits us in the twenty-first century.

Fr. Jack Estes, Rector
St. Luke's Anglican Church
Bakersfield, CA, USA

Conclusion in Part

The resolution and call to act above form a natural conclusion to "a statement of beliefs with the purpose of inciting action" within the Anglican Communion, and it is tempting to simply stop here. Yet, to complete the thesis of this work as stated in the beginning, this is precisely where we must not stop. For the Anglican Manifesto, while first addressing the issues in its own house, is designed to go beyond denominational lines.

Once a revived Fellowship of Anglican Churches has been established, they in turn share the potential to become a catalyst for a revived and reunified Fellowship of Christian Churches worldwide. Thus, in order to cross the finish line, *Anglican Manifesto* must take us through the theological basis for reunification, as well as the practical applications and procedures required by such an endeavor. In short, how will this work out in the real world within the context of the emerging oneworld era.

What follows then might be considered *Manifesto* part 2, the description of an Anglican catalyst in effecting a transformation to the Oneworld Church. If we are to arrive at such a destination, first we must formulate a theological position which may allow for the breadth of Christian expressions to find common ground, and a means of fellowship among one another. The next chapter reflects an assertion of an answer to this quest to be found in what I will call the Sacramental Principle. In the concluding chapter on the Oneworld Era, we will consider the final applications for the Anglican Manifesto.

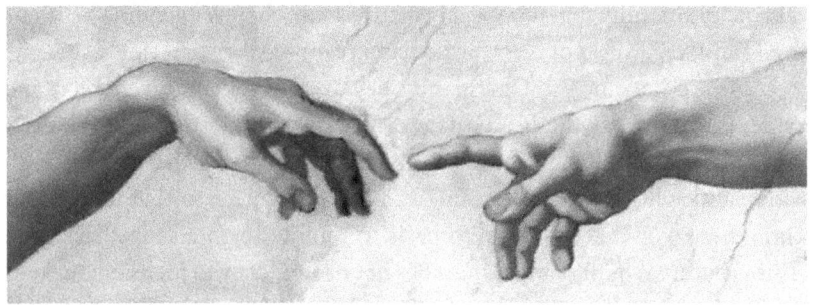

An outward visible sign, of an inward spiritual reality

—CATECHISM BCP

6

The Sacramental Principle

HAVING ESTABLISHED THE THEOLOGICAL dynamics present in the Anglican-Ism of our time, and the spiritual conflict that has ensued, let us move on to consider how the Anglican Communion itself represents a microcosm of the whole of Christianity. For indeed, the crisis that Anglicans now find themselves immersed in is a conflict which is happening across the spectrum of the church—denominations and non-denominations alike. It just happens to be particularly visible within the Anglican stream. Due to this visibility, and the fact that the Anglican Church is the church of the Via Media, the middle way, Anglicans may be uniquely positioned to serve as a catalyst in the reunification of the Christian church at large—a desire of many through the ages which has proved to be elusive at best.

The issues we have discussed that are present and active in the midst of the current Anglican angst, are indicative of a much broader problem confronting Christianity in general. The growing resiliency of the liberal vision under the guise of Christian love is in harmony with the prevailing value system of the oneworld era. As such, a pseudo "Christianity" is on the rise, with theological variations that make it readily available to merge with the religions of the world. To counter this movement we must discern a principle of unity that may be affirmed as true wherever genuine believers are found, regardless of their particular stream of Christian expression.

As we have noted, Christianity began as a solitary river, deep and wide, flowing from the headwaters of Christ, the apostles, and the early councils of the church. Flowing down through history that river has divided and split into major streams and minor rivulets, so that now in our time there would seem to be no basis to reunite them all together again. This is because, by and large, churches have a tendency to focus on one part of the gospel to the exclusion of others. What is most important to your church: preaching and teaching; feeding the poor; evangelism; sacraments; prophesy and healing? As Christians we polarize around that which we deem vital and find most comfortable, that portion of the gospel in which we relate to. Our worship develops from there and takes on qualities which enhance and reaffirm our position. However, over time as our particular emphases develop independently from one another, they also may become unrecognizable to our fellow Christians who are immersed in their own streams. The divide across the spectrum appears so great, and the expressions so seemingly different, that at times there are genuine followers of Jesus who do not think that others are even Christian, or part of the body of Christ—the church.

Fine and dandy! Let everyone go their own way. But wait! Now an imposter has grown up in our midst. Pseudo "Christianity" has the potential to take over all of us. The Anglican Church is currently fighting for our life, whether we fully realize it yet or not. Your Christian church, of whatever expression, is also caught in the matrix of the spirit of the age, which is exerting pressure to yield to a new reality, whether you realize it or not. This conflict has come to all who declare, "Jesus Christ is Lord," according to the original meaning of the words.

In order to see through the polarization, and find a principle of spiritual unity, we must discern the essence of faith that is common to all. The essence present within each stream of Christian expression that in fact gives definition to the whole. Like invisible ink that can suddenly be seen under a ultraviolet light, we must find a theological lens to look through that will open our eyes and our understanding to see the spiritual reality that is present among all believers. Sacramental theology is the means by which we can look beneath the reflections on the surface. An expanded sacramental understanding is the lens by which we can see the unity of the church in all the expressions across the spectrum.

The Sacramental Principle

If you are reading this from within the Anglican, Roman Catholic, or Orthodox expressions, the language of sacrament will be very familiar. Others, who are in the evangelical, charismatic, or non-denominational streams, may barely even know of the concept. The language of sacrament may be unfamiliar to you. Regardless of the level of familiarity, we will all need to expand our understanding to a deeper level, in order to gain clarity of the principle that binds us together. The principle that is able to provide the means of unity for the church in the twenty-first century. The Sacramental Principle.

Simply put, the Sacramental Principle describes the action of the transcendent God, becoming immanent through elements within the physical world. God interacts with the world and with his people through the means of a sacramental process. The various expressions of Christian faith each connect with God through a part of that process. Although vibrant in and of themselves, each exists as part of the whole. The whole is bound together by the sacramental nature of the universe and God's interaction with it.

A Sacramental Worldview

Whenever we begin a discussion about sacraments, we must acknowledge that there is a limit to what can be known. This is because sacraments by their very nature bring us into close contact with God. We encounter God by means of the sacrament. In this encounter there resides a mystery which cannot be fully sorted out by our finite understanding. Yet, there is much which we can affirm as true based upon Scripture, tradition, and reason which are the classical sources of authority in the Anglican-Ism. Chiefly, that God has ordained the sacraments as a way of conveying his grace into our lives. In reality, creation itself is sacramental by nature.

What exactly is a sacrament?

What are we describing when we use the term sacramental?

What takes place in the experience of a sacramental moment?

The classic definition of sacrament is "an outward visible sign of an inward spiritual reality."[1] Naturally, this description can be rather cryptic, especially to those who are formed in a different theological context. The key words here are "visible" and "spiritual reality." A sacrament is something that makes the spiritual reality of God, his person, his presence, and his love visible to us here in the world.

1. From the Book of Common Prayer.

Anglican Manifesto

God is love. God is holy. God is spirit. In a word God is transcendent. He is above, beyond, separate from the created order in which we live and move and have our being. And yet, God is actively engaged with his creation and in particular with the men and women created in his image. The transcendent one becomes immanently present and available by means of the sacraments, or more correctly through a sacramental process. He becomes visible, even tangible, and we experience his person with us in a spiritual reality. I will argue that this is taking place throughout the whole of the Christian church, regardless of what stream of expression one finds himself/herself immersed in. Simply put, the sacramental nature of God's interaction with his people is the way in which he touches our lives.

God touches our lives through elements in the physical world. In the water of Baptism God touches us and joins our lives with his. In the bread and wine of communion God touches and nourishes our spirits. In fact, all of creation is available to God to use sacramentally, as an instrument to touch our lives and make himself known. "The earth is the Lord's and and the fullness thereof . . ."[2] Once we grasp this, we are on our way to developing a sacramental worldview—a worldview that has the potential to bring together and heal the disjointed body of Christ.

The mystery of the sacraments may be depicted as God infusing elements of the physical world with the spiritual reality of his presence. Several things happen when this occurs. First, God's presence is manifested. We encounter the invisible God in the tangible world in which we live. Next, as a result of this encounter a stronger bond or connection is formed; as individuals we form a bond both with him and with the community of believers. Of course, the primary example of this is Jesus himself. Through faith in Christ a sacramental connection is made unto salvation. In the incarnation the spiritual reality of God became tangible in the person of Christ, being made visible through Jesus' physical body. Finally, as we participate in the sacraments, we receive the benefits of his love, being strengthened within our own spirits.

That strength which God imparts to us through the sacraments is known as grace. Exactly what grace is and what grace accomplishes has been a matter of debate throughout the history of Christianity. Is grace a transforming power, or simply something that enables us to see ourselves as God's children? Is grace infused in us by God—like a doctor giving a shot—or is it something he makes available, but we must access through

2. Ps 24:1.

The Sacramental Principle

our participation? How we understand the answers to these questions affects our understanding of the nature of the sacraments. The theological position we take then becomes evident in the practical ordering of the sacraments in the life of the community.

So, when we talk of sacrament we are referring to the process by which the transcendent, Holy God, becomes immanent and present to us by manifesting himself by means of something in the created order; something that, in fact, he created to begin with. We can observe this principle at work throughout the Holy Scripture in both the Old and New Testaments, and indeed, is at the very heart of God's plan of salvation.

While maintaining a special preeminence for the sacraments of Baptism and Holy Eucharist, we must not limit the sacramental nature of the universe to these two foci. In developing a sacramental principle it is critical that we acknowledge a dynamic understanding of God's interaction with his creation. God is not limited to simply two sacraments as a means of revealing himself, although it is clear that they have been given special emphasis in the life of the Church. By embracing a grander sacramental understanding, we find that all of the natural order becomes available to God as a means of imparting his love and grace. The whole world is available to God as a vessel to manifest his presence.

Biblical examples of this principle abound in both Old and New Testaments. The burning bush and Moses, Aaron's staff, the prophets, the temple itself, and perhaps even the practice of sacrifice and feasts are all examples found in the Old Testament. In them God facilitates encounter with his people by infusing some part of the natural order with his divine power and presence. The results of such encounters vary according to the response of the people who participate in them. The Old Testament experience of God is one of the direct presence of God's person, knowledge, and power to those who trust and serve him.

In the New Testament, Jesus himself is the paradigm for sacrament. "He is the radiance of the glory of God and the exact imprint of his nature . . ."[3] His flesh was a vessel of light, yet he also participated in the more widespread sacramental nature of the world in relationship to God: turning water into wine, establishing Baptism and the Eucharist, anointing blind eyes with spit and dust; walking on water. The healing passages in particular demonstrate the wide variety of means in the natural through which

---

3. Heb 1:3.

God touches the lives of his people with healing power: laying on of hands, washing in pools or rivers, handkerchiefs, and even the spoken word.

Perhaps, the sacramental quality of God's interaction with his people is no where better observed than in the motif of the temple. The biblical nature of this sacramental worldview is on display throughout each phase, beginning with the Ark of the Covenant in the tabernacle and through to its completion in the new heaven and earth. The temple itself is the icon of heaven touching earth, the transcendent God becoming visible, tangible, and immanent in the midst of his people. A wonderful example is found in Solomon's dedication of the temple in Jerusalem, when the cloud of God's glory became visible, his presence tangible, and no one could stand as a result. Certainly, this was a sacramental moment.

In the Old Testament, God touches his people through the inanimate structure of the temple, and the organic elements of the sacrifices in worship. With the advent of Christ in the New Testament, Jesus becomes the living temple here on earth. God touches his people through the human body of his son, and the ultimate sacrifice of worship on the cross. This sacramental interaction continues to unfold as the Holy Spirit is poured out upon all believers. The church becomes the organic temple, comprised of "living stones." When the church assembles, God touches his people in the midst of their fellowship. Finally, God's plan of salvation is complete. There is no longer any need for the temple, for God dwells among his people, and is with them face to face for eternity. Sacrament has become salvation.

The Sacraments Proper

While living as, and being, a sacrament to the world at large, the church has also discerned this sacramental nature of God's interaction in their midst. Correspondingly, there are capital S sacraments that have been established. Not only as a means to effect a connection with God, but also in recognition of the one that is already present. Protestant churches in the Reformed and Lutheran steams, as well as the Anglicans, recognize two official sacraments: Baptism and Holy Eucharist, or Communion. They point to these two as instituted by Jesus himself in the gospel accounts. Another stream of Protestant churches issuing from the Reformation, namely the Anabaptists, declare three sacraments instituted by Jesus: Baptism, Communion, and Footwashing.

The Sacramental Principle

The Roman Catholic Church has taken a more expanded view to begin with, since sacramental worship is their primary emphasis. Catholics affirm seven sacraments: (1) Baptism; (2) Eucharist; (3) Penance—confession; (4) Anointing for healing; (5) Confirmation; (6) Ordination; (7) Marriage. These are the sacraments proper, but even further allowance is made for recognition of the sacramental quality of everyday faith and prayer. Actions and events which also convey a sense of God's presence in our lives are called sacramentals. It is interesting to note that many in the early church held to a more expanded list of sacraments. St. Augustine of Hippo affirmed thirty sacraments. The Eastern Orthodox may wish to include a sacramental quality to icons, which are paramount in their liturgical worship.

The concept of sacramentals recognizes that God's interaction with his people, the way he touches our lives, extends beyond the core sacraments that we acknowledge at the heart of worship as a community. God brings the spiritual reality of his presence to us in the midst of our regular lives. Blessings for meals, persons, and places have a sacramental quality, perhaps through the words spoken; the physical sign of the cross enacted; or the sprinkling of "holy water." These form a connection with the Holy Spirit. Also, in the elements of "popular piety," the lighting of a candle in prayer, a meditation with the rosary, processions, and even dance. There is recognition that God may chose to become visible through anything which is available in the physical world, as a channel of communication to his people.[4]

In general the church has described the nature of the sacraments in one of three ways: (1) Grace; (2) Remembrance; (3) Real Presence. These are not necessarily mutually exclusive, but taken together may create a fusion understanding to contemplate the sacramental life. The reader will note my intention to integrate vital elements of faith and practice. This intentionality is found throughout the book.

Once in a seminary class our professor asked, "What is grace?" My friend shot up his hand and said, "Grace is God's unmerited favor given to us through Christ." I also responded, "Grace is his enabling power that flows from his life into our own." The wise professor said, "Good. Put the two together and you will have a good beginning of a definition for grace."

Through the sacramental interaction with his people, God grants us favor. That is his loving kindness, forgiveness of our offenses, acceptance as his sons and daughters, even joy and delight in who he has made us to be, and who we are becoming through faith in him. Unmerited favor

---

4. See *Catechism of the Catholic Church* at http://www.scborromeo.org/ccc.htm.

means we cannot earn grace through our own efforts, to more or less present an invoice to God for grace in return for good behavior. Although to be fair, Roman Catholics do have an understanding of merit that is imparted through participation in the redemptive suffering of Christ, and his ongoing work in the world.

Grace as enabling power recognizes our great need for God's strength as we face the trials and temptations of this life. Jesus promised, "I will never leave you nor forsake you."[5] He sent the Holy Spirit to lead us in all truth. Grace is the supernatural power God imparts to us, so that we can overcome our weaknesses and the assaults of the world about us. Then we are made able to walk in his ways and delight in his will. His grace gives us the strength to stand in the midst of the challenges, assaults, and even tragedies that we all face on our journey through this world.

As noted earlier, Catholics may have the most developed sacramental understanding as part of their spiritual formation. Nevertheless, they seem to confine grace to the seven sacraments—capital S. In developing this sacramental worldview, I will press for further expansion, allowing that grace may come through any sacramental moment. Thus, God's unmerited favor and enabling power flow into our lives from every quarter.

Throughout all of Christendom, if there is any understanding of sacrament or communion, it is found in the form of remembrance. Evangelicals often cite passages from the Lord's Supper or 1 Corinthians in sharing the bread and wine, or juice, in remembrance of Jesus, as he directed. This may be a more superficial notion of remembrance, but even so calls for the church to give pause, be together, hearken back and remember, take note of what Jesus has done for us. Even at this level, remembrance is a valid and positive spiritual exercise.

In actuality, there is a deeper meaning associated with remembrance, one that is found upon closer examination of the Greek text of Scripture. When Jesus breaks the bread and gives the cup to his disciples at the last supper, he says to them, "Do this in remembrance of me."[6] The word used there, *anamnesis*, is a particular verb tense in Greek that signifies an ongoing real action. Remembrance is bringing that event, that action, from the past forward into the present, where it becomes real once again. As real as when it first took place. This is the remembrance of sacrament.

---

5. Heb 13:5.
6. Luke 22:19.

The Sacramental Principle

Anglicans understand and describe the nature of sacrament in terms of real presence. This Anglican doctrine speaks of the spiritual reality of the presence of Christ in the celebration of the Eucharist, and continues the theme of the sacraments as a means of relationship with God. How wonderful and mysterious this is, that the eternal, awesome, living God would manifest himself through elements of his creation. The sacraments form a virtual lifeline from the eternal kingdom of God to the very temporal present in which we live. In doing so the community of believers in Jesus Christ is nurtured and sustained, and we are commissioned to work with God to further his kingdom in this world.

From the beginning of the Anglican-Ism, Thomas Cranmer sought out the middle ground which retained the essence of the mystery of the Eucharist, but refocused his theology onto the celebration of the community. In doing so, the choice was made in between transubstantiation, the doctrine that declares the bread and wine literally become the flesh and blood of Christ, and the strictly memorial viewpoint asserted by Zwingli and the Anabaptists groups, who understood communion more as a simple acknowledgement of something that had happened in the past.

I would encourage us all to affirm that there is a mystery taking place in the sacrament of Holy Eucharist, in the waters of Baptism, in the seven sacraments, and in every sacramental moment; God is present—spiritually present. Heaven and earth are touching. We may not be able to explain exactly how, or point to the exact moment when it begins or ends, but it is nonetheless real, spiritually real, in a way that is more concrete and lasting than the material world around us. Real presence puts us in proximity with God's person. A connection is being made, a sacramental connection through which our lives are joined with his life. His life flows through that connection into our life. The process of that flow, and the way we perceive it, is what we shall consider next in the development of the Sacramental Principle.

The sacramental understanding of God's interaction with humanity is found woven into the very fabric of Scripture, and finds expression in the life of God's people. Thereby, the biblical worldview is virtually synonymous with a sacramental worldview. Both stand together in answering the questions of God and mankind, sin and salvation, Spirit and church with the same consistency. The sacramental worldview developed here only turns the focus a little deeper, to express biblical truths through the underlying essence. To complete our work here we must further develop our understanding of how the sacramental nature of the universe can become a principle in operation that works to join the various streams of Christianity back together into one. The church was one at the council of Nicaea, and then splintered and diversified down through history. Now is the time to reverse the process—the streams and rivulets running back together to make one River of God on the earth.

Let us consider once again more deeply the question, "What happens in a sacrament or in a sacramental moment?" Upon reflection we will apply our answers to basic models of communication and onward toward the development of a new epistemology—that is, the way in which we attain knowledge. From this exercise, we will then extract the Sacramental Principle, which can be found in operation in every faithful expression of Christianity. It is this Sacramental Principle that unifies us.

Communication as Sacrament

We have established that it is through a sacramental process that God brings himself near to us, to communicate with us and to impart the knowledge of his will. This knowledge of God, his person and nature, as well as his plans and directions, are imparted in those moments when we encounter him. God speaks and we listen, and we speak and he listens in return. Our lives are joined together, like a husband and wife who join their lives together through conversation in the kitchen at the end of a busy day. They communicate with one another by talking, sharing emotions, and even through intuition. It is well known that 80 percent of all communication is nonverbal. In doing so they are all the while imparting knowledge of themselves to one another.

This kind of interpersonal communication takes on many different forms and flows through many different channels to find completion. We may speak directly, listing facts or figures, utilizing our rational capacity. We may connect through the sharing of a story, or experience, in a matrix that imparts information past and present. Communication happens intuitively without words by means of our emotions, movements and gestures. Even in ways we cannot exactly define. Each of these in turn becomes its own channel of communication, serving to impart the message we seek to convey. These channels of communication become the means by which we impart the knowledge of who we are and receive the knowledge of the ones we are close to. This is how we get to know someone.

The Sacramental Principle

In like manner, God imparts knowledge of who he is to his people through various sacramental channels of communication. By means of the sacramental process God reveals himself to us, makes himself known. This revelation can be properly understood within a model of interpersonal communication. The basic elements of communication theory also hold true in our communication with God. By applying models of understanding about the communication process we can begin to assess some of the dynamic qualities of that revelation, and then move on to apply them in our development of the Sacramental Principle.

In the simplest understanding of communication three elements are present: Sender, Message, Receiver.

Sender + *Message*   Receiver

The sender has a message, something he/she wishes to communicate to another person. In order for that message to be understood, it must be sent to the receiver in a manner that makes it possible for him to first recognize it, and then process it, and finally understand the meaning. Communication has been successful, once the message has been received.

In order for the sender to get the message to the receiver there must be a means of delivery, a channel by which to send it. So, the sender encodes a message, chooses a particular channel—i.e., verbal, written, etc., and sends it to the receiver.

Sender→*Message*→----------------------------------Receiver
                                      Channel

Once the message has been received and understood, it becomes part of the knowledge of the one who has received it. The message has been transferred from sender to receiver, and the act of communication has been successful.

Sender   Receiver+*Message*

While this is the ideal with all communication, the message may in fact never reach the intended receiver. Along the way it may run into interference either from without in the environment, or from within such as the receiver being distracted by his own thoughts. Interference in the form of external or internal factors may combine to thwart the process. In regards to sacramental communication from God, interference will remain fairly consistent throughout our discussion. Primarily it may be defined as that which has always resisted the gospel: the world, the flesh, and the devil. Interference may manifest itself externally, as in through social pressure, or internally, as in lustful desire or pride. Further interference may also be calculated and systematically exercised by demonic powers and principalities.

Sender→ *Message*→--------------XXX   Receiver
               Channel   *Interference*

One further element that is important to interject at this point is the idea of the messenger. This was much more prevalent in antiquity than with modern communication technology. Often, a king, for example, would entrust his message to a faithful servant who would then travel to the appointed receivers. Once there, the servant would choose the appropriate channel for communication, one that would overcome cultural and linguistic barriers. The prophets are a prime example of messengers sent by God, their physical bodies becoming sacramental channels for God. Today pastors and priests continue in this communication mode, but it is not limited to the ordained, all of God's people are available to be his conduits wherever he has placed them.

Sender--------→--------*Message*-----→-----------Receiver

Naturally, our discussion above culminates in the person of Jesus Christ. Since Jesus is the ultimate sacrament, the "express image of the invisible God," he is also God's ultimate means of communication. In the person of Jesus resides God's greatest revelation to mankind. The power of revelation becomes evident through understanding that Christ is at one and the same time messenger, message, and channel: as the Son of God, he is messenger; as the Word of God, he is message; as a man, he is the channel. God is the sender and we are the receivers.

God----→-------*Jesus Christ*------→------------Humanity

It is true that Jesus, as the Living Word, is no longer physically present with us. Yet, one can argue that due to the creative power of God's Word there resides an archetype, a concrete essence, of the spiritual Word of God

The Sacramental Principle

within the natural realm. There are multiple channels available to God to bring his presence and his word into our lives. These channels when enlivened by the Spirit convey his person and messages to us. The process of God's communication through these channels is sacramental in quality. This is communication as sacrament.

Finally, while being careful to maintain the distinction which God has placed upon certain elements as primary channels of revelation—i.e., the Bible and the sacraments, we have laid the groundwork for expansion of additional channels for the flow of his grace within the context of a sacramental worldview. As shown below God is not limited to simply one or two channels by which to communicate with us.

```
                        Channel -------→---------------
Sender→ Message         Channel--------→--------------- Receiver
                        Channel--------→---------------
```

This is what is taking place when we partake of the sacraments, or participate in the sacramental process: a channel of communication is formed that connects the thoughts and heart of God with the thoughts and hearts of men and women. But more than just an exchange of ideas takes place; this sacramental connection brings an impartation of God's presence, his person and all of his attributes. The grace of God flows into our lives. This is nothing short of revelation in the purest sense of the word. The transcendent God reveals himself, becomes real, tangible in the physical world where he can be known. When we as human being stand in this kind of sacramental connection and are receivers of the revelation that takes place, we are changed by it—transformed within our own hearts, minds and souls. The result is knowledge of God.

Having established the basis of communication as sacrament, we may now move to a consideration of the particular channels the Lord has made available to communicate with us. Since this sacramental communication brings with it the knowledge of God, we must also examine the ways in which we are designed to receive knowledge. In moving toward a new epistemology, I wish to identify the various faculties within us to attain knowledge. Then the next step will be taken which correlates the available channels to the various faculties within our being by which we ascertain knowledge. In this we will see how particular channels are designed for particular faculties of reception, and how we tend to polarize around certain combinations in our respective church communities.

The Sacramental Principle

The Christian church has long affirmed the doctrine and practice of sacrament, even if there has been some discussion about the exact meanings involved. God extends himself through his creation; he touches our lives by means of the bread and wine of communion, the waters of baptism, and anything and everything else which happens to be available to him at the time. When we perceive his touch, we engage in the knowledge that God is revealing to us about himself, by means of the various faculties within our being. Faculties created by God so that we may attain knowledge of him and the universe. This outward visible sign of an inward spiritual reality comprises the essence of the Sacramental Principle.

The sacramental nature of creation resides at the heart of the biblical world view. This principle is the heartbeat that pumps the lifeblood of relationship with God throughout all the members of the body. That includes the various fellowships of the Christian church: Catholic, Orthodox, Anglican, Protestant, Evangelical, Charismatic, and Independent. Like the blood flowing beneath the surface of our skin, this sacramental reality also flows beneath the surface of our common life, and often remains out of view, or unrecognized, by the various parts of the body it supplies. When, or if, all the fellowships which comprise the body of Christ can appropriate a clear understanding of how our lives are joined with God in a sacramental manner, the possibility is opened for all to be reunited in the heart of the biblical world view.

In order to provide a matrix for this type of reunification it is necessary to explain clearly how each of the vibrant expressions of faith found in the major streams of Christianity—Catholic, Evangelical, Charismatic, and Liberal—are all sacramental in nature.[7] They are distinct from one another only as parts of a whole.

Humanity is designed to receive the knowledge of God sacramentally, through the faculties he has placed within us. These faculties of knowledge align with God's sacramental conduits to form channels of communication that result in the knowledge of God and of his kingdom. By extension, communities of church expression have polarized around particular sacramental channels, and thereby created barriers between one another. These barriers fall away when each expression is more clearly recognized as

---

7. Please note that the use of the term "Liberal" above refers to the expression of faith that maintains the genuine, authentic portion of the gospel concerned with the welfare of the poor, the oppressed and disenfranchised: the Real Liberal.

a valid part of the whole. Therefore the Sacramental Principle becomes the means of reunification of the Christian church universal.

How do we know, or experience such a phenomena? What are the implications for adopting, or reclaiming, such a theological premise for the life of the Church? How does the Sacramental Principle fit within the context of a biblical worldview?

Our understanding of God can be most fully realized through the integration of the components within the Sacramental Principle, beginning with an expanded epistemology—the study of knowledge and how we attain it. Such integration has the potential to enliven the church for mission and ministry, as we exponentially increase the means to apprehend God and the blessing of his presence. In order to consider what such integration may look like, we must first clearly define a sacramental understanding for our present context, in contrast to various modern theological positions. Next, we must move toward a new epistemology, which formulates a more complete understanding of the faculties within a human being. Faculties designed for the attaining of knowledge. Finally, the correlation of sacrament (God moving toward man) and epistemology (mankind receiving knowledge of God) will meld into the theological basis for the Sacramental Principle that will, in turn, provide a foundation for Christian fellowship. Once the base has been established, we can then consider the practical outworking of such a theology in the life of the church.

Because the Bible presents God as both beyond the world and present to the world, theologians in every era are confronted with the challenge of articulating the Christian understanding of the nature of God in a manner that balances, affirms and holds in creative tension the twin truths of the divine transcendence and the divine immanence. A balanced affirmation of both truths facilitates a proper relation between theology and culture. Where such balance is lacking, serious theological problems readily emerge. Hence an overemphasis on transcendence can lead to a theology that is distant, removed, and irrelevant to the cultural context in which it seeks to speak. Whereas an overemphasis on immanence can produce a theology indistinct, immersed, and held captive to a specific culture. Both are ineffective in conveying the fullness of God's revelation to the world.

Therefore, in developing the Sacramental Principle we must take care to strive for balance. The temptation will be stronger to err toward the side of immanence, as we seek to encounter God directly and to know him both cognitively and experientially. Historically, our understanding of transcendence and immanence has progressed through several stages. Some explanation of these stages needs to be touched upon before attempting to depict the Sacramental Principle. The stages can be identified in correlation to the historical paradigm shifts and the theological responses to them.

During the turn from the premodern era into the Enlightenment with its emphasis on reason and scientific fact, theologians promoted the idea that there are two realms of reality—the spiritual realm beyond human perception, and the physical realm which surrounds our daily existence. The knowledge attainable by human beings is limited to the empirical data found only in the physical realm. This hypothesis demanded a distinction between objects present in the experience of the human knower and objects lying beyond experience, which could not be known. This barrier became known as the Kantian Void, after Emmanuel Kant, who developed this idea.

```
 Heaven                         Θ
 ───────────────────────────────────────────── Kantian Void
 Earth               Humanity
```

**Construct of modern theology separating the knowable earth
and the unknowable heaven
Θ, the symbol used above to signify God,
is the first letter in the Greek word θηοσ, or Theos**

So, Kant envisioned a gulf between the material world which we know by use of our senses, and the spiritual realm, where the transcendent God dwelt. The problem being that there is no way to cross the gulf, since our only faculty for knowledge was through the empirical senses, and the use of reason by the mind to make sense of the data. God and his transcendence are cut off from mankind, who find themselves alone in the material world. Perhaps Kant would have appreciated the song by Madonna, "I am a material girl, living in a material world." Any inward spiritual reality was in fact imperceptible.

Kant's schema left mankind ultimately cut off from God, and the importance of religious endeavor lessened through the period of the Enlightenment. The denial of the immanent quality of God's nature resulted in a mere caricature of his person. God was banished to the realm of original creator, a watchmaker that put in all in motion, but now is off somewhere else, ceasing concern and relationship with humanity. By overemphasizing God's transcendence, Kant erected a solid wall between heaven and earth, thus eliminating the possibility of experiential knowledge of God. Deism is a good example of this understanding put into effect. God is out there somewhere creating, but has little interest or ongoing connection with the human experience.[8]

In seeking to reestablish a place for God in the modern era, Freidrich Schleiermacher repositioned God back into the realm of human experience. Schleiermacher asserted that our knowledge of God is based on our subjective experience of him. God is purely immanent, and because of this he is known only through intuition, or "feeling," he is therefore shielded from scrutiny from rational scholars, like Kant, armed with the weapons of historical-critical method and modern philosophy.

However, as we have discussed, by discarding any standard of objective truth found either in Scripture or in reason, the new liberal theology also severely truncated the transcendent character of God's being. In doing so, Schleiermacher's theology gave place for the experience of humanity to determine the nature of the divine. Subjective experience became the standard of authority, rather than objective propositions—such as those found in Scripture. Not surprisingly the liberal stream that followed soon began crafting God after their own image. God became a human construct. What was felt to be true regarding God became authoritative, with no objective standard of appeal outside our own experience. God was now to be found only within creation, leaving any transcendent distinction null and void. The wall continued to exist, only now God was locked out of heaven and to be found only within the physical realm.

The Schleiermacher school of thought was answered at the turn of the century by one of the greatest theologian of the twentieth century, Karl Barth. As a pastor, Barth became fed up with the liberal theology he had been schooled in. Returning to the authority of Scripture, Barth declared that God is utterly transcendent—he is "wholly other." Barth criticized liberal theology for turning the gospel into a religious message that tells humans of their own divinity instead of recognizing it as the Word of God. In essence Barth was calling for a revolution in theological method, a theology "from above" to replace the old, human-centered theology "from below." Throughout his *Church Dogmatics*, he emphasized the wholly otherness of God, the gospel, eternity and salvation. These great truths, he argued,

---

8. Grenz and Olson, *20th Century Theology*, 11–12.

cannot be built up from universal human experience or reason, but must be received in obedience from God's revelation.[9]

According to Barth, the only way we know God is through his mighty acts demonstrated in history. God chooses to break in on humanity according to his own times and purposes. Of course, the greatest act of all is the coming of Jesus Christ. He is the paradigm around which all of human history revolves. God resides in the spiritual realm of the heavens, breaking into the physical realm of the earth to accomplish his purposes at specific points in time.

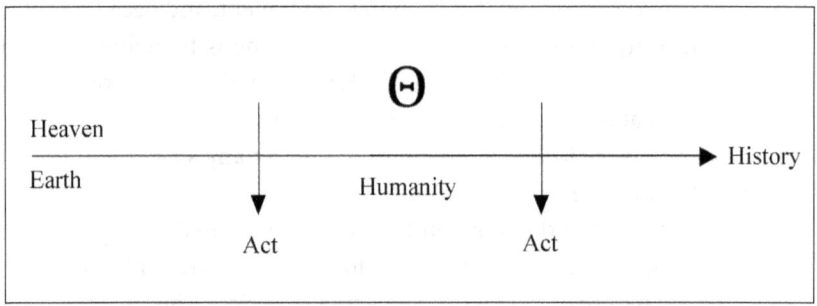

God interposes his will thru mighty acts that break in from heaven to earth

Moving toward the postmodern era, the pendulum swings back to the side of immanence, in a synthesis of new thought first developed in a novel philosophical system known as process theology. The early champion of process thought was the philosopher Alfred North Whitehead. In Whitehead's view God is inextricably connected to creation. God, creation, and mankind are all together in the process of becoming. Process theology differs from the more ancient pantheism, which purports a divine being, or beings, residing within the earth, or parts of the created world. Instead of God being in creation, Whitehead proposes that creation is in God, pan-en-theism. Together they are in process growing, changing, interacting, and this process constitutes the ultimate nature of reality. This metaphysic of process leads Whitehead to a specific theological orientation. Three postulates provide a summary of this theology:

First, God is neither aloof from, nor unaffected by, the world; rather God and the world are interdependent. Whitehead's emphasis, therefore, clearly is on the divine immanence, for God is "an actual entity immanent in the actual world."

9. Grenz and Olson, *20th Century Theology*, 22–67.

The Sacramental Principle

Second, God works in the world primarily through persuasion, rather than coercion. God provides the lure, of course, but each occasion has the prerogative to accept or reject it. Thus, when Whitehead offered images of God and the world, the two he chose were "tender care" and "infinite patience."

Third, we ought not to view God in terms of omnipotence, but as the one who suffers with the world. Whitehead rejected the classical understanding of God as the divine, choosing instead a God sublime.[10] Thus, Whitehead's process theology is attempting to balance the transcendent and the immanent by removing any distinction between the two, and containing all within the realm of the physical universe.

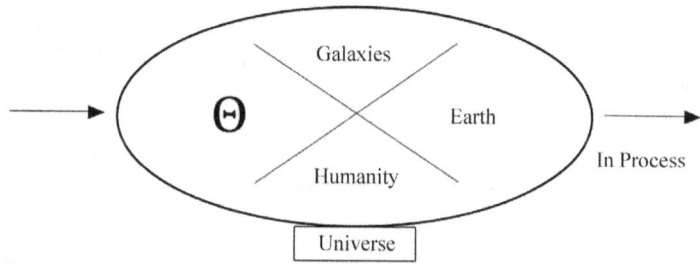

**God, cosmos and mankind in process of becoming
Interactively contained within the physical universe
Monism or Panentheism**

The uber immanence of process fits the postmodern paradigm of the interconnectedness of everything in the universe. God becomes the force of Star Wars, joined together with humanity and the universe all in all. Naturally, this is counter to God's revelation through the Holy Scripture which clearly delineates the separation between the creature and the creator.

For the Sacramental Principle to be effective, both the transcendent and immanent aspects of God must be apprehended and fused together without sacrificing the integrity of either. Then we can take the next step of understanding this Principle at work in the church.

In the biblical worldview, Kant's separation between heaven and earth remains intact. There is a clear distinction between the two, yet, rather than being separated by an impossible gulf, the barrier may be thought of more accurately as a thin, ephemeral curtain. Barth is right. God is wholly other, and at times he does invade human history through mighty acts. Yet, this

---

10. Whitehead, as summarized by Grenz and Olson, *20th Century Theology*, 132–38.

does not preclude the light of his presence, love, and grace from flowing into the created realm in a more subtle and continuous manner. Ironically, Whitehead's process theology may offer some insights, as it depicts a system of dynamic interaction between God and the world. Yet, orthodoxy must maintain a different set of criteria by which to compose such an interaction. While all of creation is present before God, he remains distinct—God is not dependent upon creation to complete the process of his becoming. Rather all of creation is dependent upon him, and available to him to utilize in order to manifest his presence and purposes.

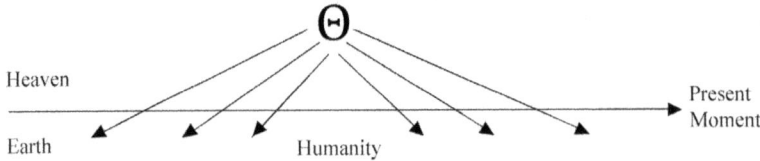

God brings the light of his presence from heaven to earth
Acting in the moments he chooses

The sacraments of the church (Eucharist/Baptism) are particular examples of the flow of God's presence, love, and grace into the created realm. The sacraments exemplify the power of the transcendent God infused into elements of the natural order. They formulate an invitation to encounter with the living God. Those who participate in this invitation experience his presence, and receive his grace.

In the biblical worldview, the spiritual and the material are not in opposition to one another, but are complementary. Far from being evil, the physical is meant to be inhabited by the spiritual. We are created so as to receive life from God, who is Spirit, and to express that life through our bodies and in the physical world in which we live. The material world is created, in part, so as to make visible and manifest the realm of the invisible spirit.[11] Thus, the immanence of God is experienced and known in the sacraments. It is not by accident that the Eucharist is described by the doctrine of real presence, or that we understand grace to be imparted by means of the sacraments. These doctrines are in place precisely because they describe at least in part, the effects of the mystery of God's interaction with mankind.

---

11. See Foster, *Streams of Living Water*.

The Sacramental Principle

Having established the unlimited nature of God's sacramental action, we need to take a step back and realize that while all channels are open to him, there are certain channels that are the most consistently consistently utilized. Because we are symbolic beings, the flow of God's presence, from transcendent to immanent—heaven to earth—is channeled through the symbols which God has designated for this purpose. As Leanne Payne writes:

> The Judeo-Christian Scriptures are at once the repository and the great guardian of the Christian world picture—that is, the sacramental symbolic system. A found understanding of the Scriptures therefore evokes true imagery within the heart, just as it grants a sound theology to the mind. The way mankind in general or the individual heart images God is judged to be adequate or inadequate, true or false, as it lines up with the way the Scriptures image God . . . we are mythic beings: we live by and in our symbols. Man is an animal who symbolizes, who talks. (To talk is to symbolize. Language itself is symbol.) Thus man is set apart from the rest of the natural creation. Symbols bind up reality for us.[12]

Symbols formulate the means by which the real presence of God is manifested, and by extension the means by which we connect with him. They are visible to us in worship, the sacraments, Jesus—cross/crucifix, the Holy Scripture, community—the body of Christ, the gifts of the Spirit, and nature. These are the channels of communication that God himself has put in place, as a primary means to bring revelation into our lives. Thus, our final understanding of a sacramental world view maintains the transcendent God manifesting himself in the created realm by means of the symbols, or channels of communication, he has brought into being there.

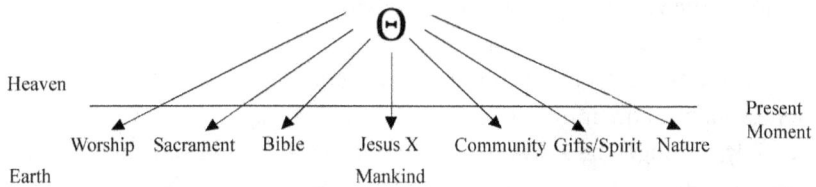

**Symbolic channels of communication allow the flow of God's real presence
To be communicated to mankind from heaven to earth
X is the first letter in the Greek word for Christ—Χριςτοσ, or Cristos**

12. Payne, *Healing Presence*, 139–40.

The pure clear light of God comes into our world like the warmth of the sunlight streaming through the window pane. The sun maintains its integrity and transcendence millions of miles away, but we experience the touch of its presence, the immanence, in the warmth and light that floods our home.

This brings us to the next place of our discussion. Having established the sacramental nature of reality from God's side, the question then emerges, how do we participate with and appropriate this reality? How do we attain knowledge through this kind of spiritual interaction? That is, knowledge in the ancient Hebrew meaning of the word, an intimate embrace of truth which then becomes part of our very being.

God desires to communicate with us—he is the sender. The communication comes via the channel selected—the sacramental symbols. How do we then receive, or know, the message? It is received by means of the faculties within our being designed to apprehend knowledge. Let us turn to a more comprehensive survey of these faculties, and how they interact to form knowledge within our human being. This will lead us to an expanded epistemology, which is itself the study of nature of knowledge.

Epistemology—Knowledge of God

In moving toward a new epistemology it should be clear that we must leave modernity behind. In the modern period knowledge was strictly truncated by relegating it to only two human faculties—namely, the rational and the empirical. I will argue for an expanded epistemology which asserts a number of faculties by which we receive and appropriate knowledge of God and the world around us. These are the faculties which reside within us, and compose the very nature of our human being: rational, intuitive, empirical, faith, emotional, mystical, relational.

The rational faculty is the seat of language and logic. It encompasses our thoughts and mind. The empirical faculty appropriates knowledge tangibly, through the senses; this is the physical part of our nature. Intuition apprehends the unseen realm of the Spirit, and discerns the essence of things that surround us. Perhaps our conscience could be included here.

We also attain knowledge through the emotive faculty within us. Emotional intelligence has been fairly recently recognized to be as important as rational thinking. We are emotional beings, and this is a factor in the knowledge of ourselves, of God, and the world.

The Sacramental Principle

People are designed to live in community. We are created for relationship with God and with others. I believe there resides within us an innate ability to function and draw knowledge and understanding from our interaction with those who are around us. Let us call this our relational faculty.

Faith may be the strongest faculty of all, even to the point of directing the others. Faith is a means by which we perceive spiritual realities, and derive the knowledge thereof. What, or how much, we are able to perceive depends upon the way in which we exercise of our faculty of faith. Faith lays hold of the first principles of knowledge. That is truth which is known without formal argument or proof. As Aristotle said, "We must know something without formal proof or we can know nothing at all."

The question is what do you put your faith in? At this point I wish to be clear. In Christian circles faith, or the Faith, usually refers to belief in God and in Jesus Christ. But, Christians aren't the only ones to exercise faith. For starters, any Jew or Muslim would contend for their faith in God, and indeed all other religious expressions also have faith in something. Even the atheist can be viewed as placing their faith in humanity, or, narcissistically, in themselves.

Finally, the mystical faculty is what I refer to as the direct line. Mystically we experience a deep inner knowledge that we may not be able to explain. Historically those who have developed this mystical faculty have known direct encounters with God, provided he is the one which is being focused upon. It is like an umbilical cord of light connecting us to God. As we shall see, this mystical means of knowing may be the primary connection with God in the sacraments.

By way of review, we depicted the universe in which we live in terms of a sacramental worldview. Balancing the transcendent and immanent qualities of God's divine nature, the boundary between heaven and earth is shown to be porous, a translucent curtain through which God is constantly engaged with human history and existence. The primary channels of his presence are found in the sacramental symbols of Jesus, Holy Scripture, worship, the gifts of the Spirit, sacraments, community, and nature. Finally, we are hard wired with certain faculties by which we know God and the world around us: rational, intuitive, emotional, empirical, faith, mystical, relational.

The final step in developing a comprehensive understanding of the Sacramental Principle is the correlation of the symbols through which God's presence comes with the human faculties by which we receive.

Anglican Manifesto

Returning to the communication model, God is the sender who encodes his message and sends it by means of the symbolic channels. The faculties within us act as receptors that bring us knowledge of God through each particular expression.

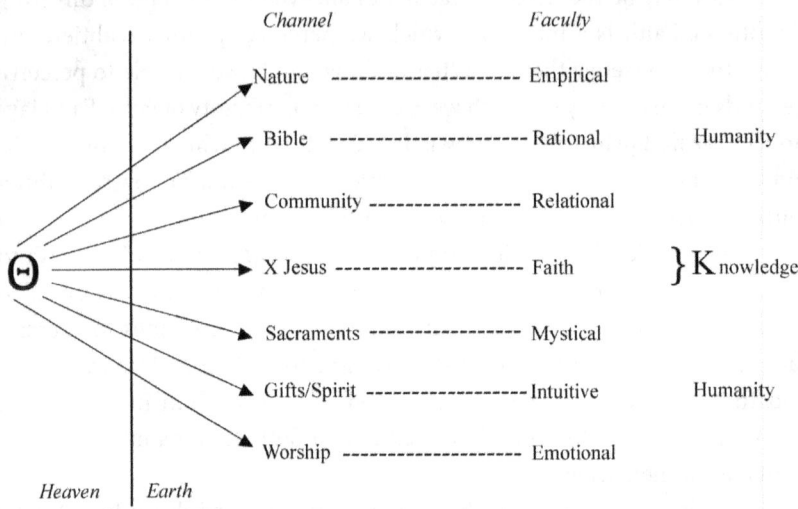

The presence of God flows from heaven to earth by means of the sacramental channels
We receive the communication from God by means of the faculties within us
The result is knowledge of God

With the empirical we know God in nature; with the rational we understand Holy Scripture; we gain knowledge of God's love in community through our relational component; by faith we lay hold of the cross; mystically we encounter God in the sacraments; the gifts of the Spirit are known by intuition; and we apprehend God in worship with our emotive being—in his presence is fullness of joy. Seven channels, seven faculties enable knowledge of God that is whole and complete. The understanding of this holistic approach to the knowledge of God has rarely been embraced by the church. Usually one or two channels are preferred to the exclusion of the others. Yet, such integration provides the means of becoming one with Christ, and becoming one with each other in the body of Christ.

None of the correlations listed in the previous illustration are to be thought of as mutually exclusive. Rather, they function more like the spectrum of color found within light, that, when fully integrated become pure and white. In like manner, the integration of God's means of communication along with our means of perception results in the sacramental reality of his life being present in us and our life being present in him. The Sacramental Principle, in its essence, is simply being in Christ, and to be in Christ is consonant with being full of the knowledge of Christ. Just as Paul wrote to the Colossians praying that, "you may be filled with the knowledge of His will in all spiritual wisdom and understanding."[13]

The Sacramental Principle describes the full integration of our life in Christ. The sacramental nature of the world, apprehended in our being, gives rise to knowledge of God incarnate in Jesus Christ. This knowledge of Christ balances the transcendent and immanent qualities of God, maintaining both his sovereignty over creation, and his availability to mankind. In the beauty of God's wisdom, this sacramental reality is given for the expansion of his kingdom. It is not an end unto itself. Rather, it depicts the filling of human vessels, which in turn overflow with the light and life of Christ into the darkness and death which currently impinge upon the temporal world.

In summary, the created world in which we live exists in a dynamic interplay with the transcendent and immanent qualities of God's being. As a result, reality is sacramental by nature. God has created us with particular faculties by which to engage with his sacramental presence and thereby to know him. The knowledge of God, his presence becoming one with our being, constitutes our being "in Christ." There are several implications for mission and ministry in the life of the church inferred by the statement above. As God's people are drawn into the understanding of his presence both in and around them, old broken ways of relating to the world, to ourselves, and to others fall away—replaced by an enlivened understanding and appropriation of the knowledge of God.

By embracing an expanded, holistic epistemology, we can discover the presence of God at work in all aspects of our humanity. Indeed, the fragmentation and polarization of much of the church results in the embracing of one channel of communication from God to the exclusion of others. God is communicating sacramentally through all the channels he has put in place through the created order. We in our church expressions are receiving his messages, but we are listening selectively, according to the channel we prefer. Thus, we are often missing other portions of the enlivening life of God as it comes to us because of the interference that rises up naturally within us, and within our respective faith communities. Hence, Catholic, Charismatic,

---

13. Col 1:9.

Anglican Manifesto

Evangelical, Liberal, and other expressions of the church remained estranged from one another, never realizing the riches they are missing.

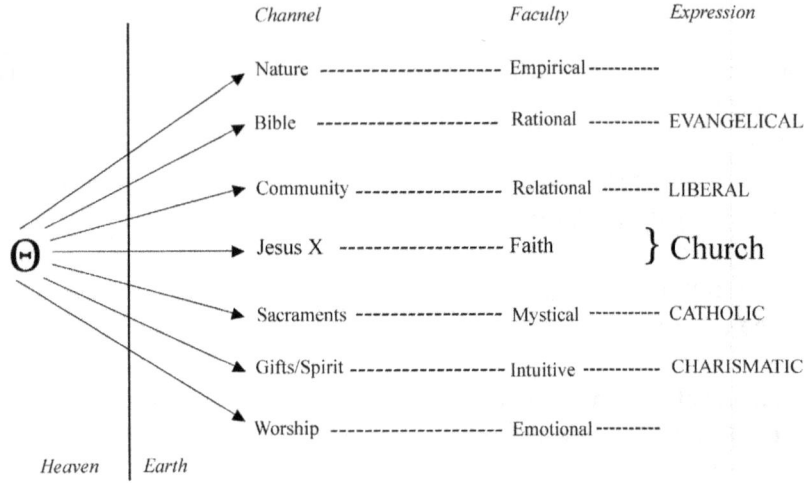

Channels and faculties through which come the flow of God's presence and knowledge Coalesce in particular expressions of church communities, often to the exclusion of others

Before we continue, please let me take a moment to clarify the ongoing use of the term "Liberal." In the previous chapters, I have explicitly made the case that the Liberal stream has departed from genuine Christian faith and practice, and in doing so now represents a pseudo Christianity in league with the spirit of the age. This Liberal vision is antithetical to the authentic beliefs which by and large remain within the other streams. But, what of the authentic liberal portion of the gospel, the part that is concerned with the poor, the oppressed, the disenfranchised, and the restoration of justice and equity in the world? Jesus himself was very concerned with these matters, and calls his church to be as well.

> Then the King will say to those on his right, "Come, you who are blessed by my Father, inherit the kingdom prepared for you from the foundation of the world. For I was hungry and you gave me food, I was thirsty and you gave me drink, I was a stranger and you welcomed me, I was naked and you clothed me, I was sick and you visited me, I was in prison and you came to me." Then the righteous will answer him, saying, "Lord, when did we see you hungry and feed you, or thirsty and give you drink? And when did we see you a stranger and welcome you, or naked and clothe you? And when did we see you sick or in prison and visit you?" And the

The Sacramental Principle

King will answer them, "Truly, I say to you, as you did it to one of the least of these my brothers, you did it to me."[14]

I have made the case that we must cast off the false liberal expression, and I stand by it. Nevertheless, let us take care not to throw the baby out with the bathwater. There remains an authentic "Liberal" stream flowing down through history, with true and vibrant elements of the faith, which we must be jealous to reclaim. It is only difficult to see it right now, as it has been largely hijacked by the false religious system. As we move forward to conclude *Manifesto*, be advised that it is this genuine, authentic, Liberal expression which I am including in the desire to bring wholeness to the church.

For practical purposes, I have identified four streams of Christian expression, or a Quad that forms a graph. These four are visible in the current landscape of the church. *Catholic, Evangelical, Charismatic,* and *Liberal* are all identities drawn from ecclesiology. An alternative rendering is made by Richard Foster. In his book *Streams of Living Water*, Foster indentifies six streams of Christian expression based more upon spiritual theology, "six dimensions of faith and practice that define Christian tradition and comprise our foundation of belief." He lifts up the enduring character of each "stream": *contemplative*—the prayer-filled life; *holiness*—the virtuous life; *charismatic*—the Spirit-empowered life; *social justice*—the compassionate life; *evangelical*—the Word-centered life; and *Incarnational*—the sacramental life. As it turns out these categories align nicely with our model of channels and faculties.[15]

---

14. Matt 25:34–40.

15. See Foster, *Streams of Living Water*.

Anglican Manifesto

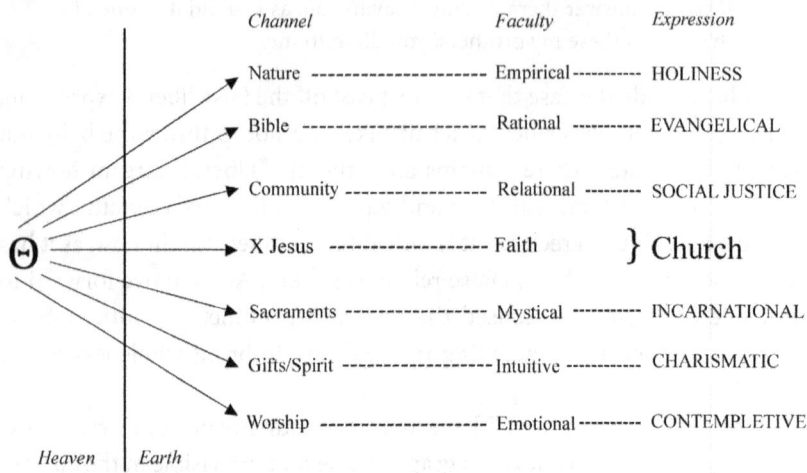

**Channels and faculties through which come the flow of God's presence and knowledge
Identified in alignment with Richard Foster's streams of Christian expression**

The mission of the church, which is to proclaim salvation in Christ, could be greatly enhanced by thinking in terms of what faculties of knowledge are in primary use by an individual or culture. Spouting rational propositions to someone who is basing their knowledge of God on mystic experience may be fruitless, and vice versa. By bearing witness to the presence of God in each particular channel, we will be able to redeem the symbols found there, and then graft them into the grander sacramental world view.

In defining the Sacramental Principle, first we recognize and affirm a sacramental worldview as consistent and true to Holy Scripture. God brings his presence and his grace from heaven to earth and into our lives by means of a sacramental process—the transcendent God becoming immanent through elements of the physical world. Through this process God communicates to his people, utilizing channels designated by him to bring the message he desires. These channels, or conduits, correspond to the faculties created with mankind by which we attain knowledge. Channel and faculty in turn fuse together over time to become an expression of Christian faith and practice, and form into a historical stream of the Christian church.

The broadcast of God's revelation is sent to our receptors, so that we may attain knowledge of him. As human beings we naturally gravitate toward the channel and faculty we are most comfortable and familiar with. We are wired this way: left-brain, right-brain; rational, intuitive; emotive,

The Sacramental Principle

sensing. We find others who are fashioned in the same way, and form church communities to fellowship together. The streams of Christianity represent personality types, ways of knowing, and modes of being together in community. God communicates to each expression one and all sacramentally. Thus, all are united in the same process.

Therefore, the Sacramental Principle is an integration, or synthesis, of sacramental theology, communication theory, epistemology, and ecclesiology. When properly applied this principle illuminates the unity of all believers in Jesus Christ. As Christ pours into us and we into him, the church is enlivened to bring healing, unity, and the proclamation of the gospel to those who are without hope in a dark age.

The Sacramental Principle begins with an understanding of God's interaction with his people, by means of a sacramental process. That is to say, he makes his presence visible through elements in the created order (physical world). This sacramental worldview is synonymous with the biblical worldview, and can be ascertained and verified in both the Old and New Testaments. The touch of God comes in those sacramental moments when he manifests, becoming visible to us in the elements of creation.

Sacramental moments are taking place in every church expression across the spectrum of Christendom, in every faithful church and denomination. The challenge is for us to first recognize that they are happening in our midst, and next, to recognize that they are happening in the midst of others who are faithful, true believers in Jesus Christ albeit different from us. This is the big challenge. Not surprisingly, the various streams of Christianity are likely to find themselves polarized around one or two modes, often to the exclusion of the others. What may be surprising is that every expression—Catholic, Evangelical, Charismatic, Real Liberal, and others—can be described and understood in relation to one another and in accordance with the Sacramental Principle. They are all found joined together on the same theological grid. This means that all have a basis from which to both maintain their identity and reform their unity.

As we move toward the conclusion of this thesis, let us consider the application of the sacramental principle within the emerging oneworld paradigm, and the answers we may expect as a result. Specifically, how does this principle in action provide for a means of communication and connection of the various Christian churches and denominations worldwide? What could begin this kind of movement toward Christian unity, and how and would the world react? Specifically, what is the role of Anglicans as agents of this kind of transformation?

Remember *Anglican Manifesto* only begins by advocating a transformation of the Anglican Communion; to complete the task we must move on to show how a revived Anglican Fellowship can become a catalyst to unite all the fellowships of the church in the oneworld era. The Anglican-Ism is a vessel rightly formed for the task, since it is the Via Media, the middle way, to begin with. In it is contained the vibrant expressions of the streams of church: Catholic, Evangelical, Charismatic, and even Real Liberal in the best sense of the term. The Anglican-Ism contains elements present in Eastern Orthodoxy, and somewhat aligned with Pentecostal, non-denominational, and Holiness movements. Taken together these are all parts of the whole of Christianity, now scattered and separated. We need only to apply the Sacramental Principle as an agent of unity, and watch the catalytic conversion that results.

I am a citizen of the world

—EVERYONE 2020

7
Oneworld Era

GLOBALIZATION. IT IS A word most of us are familiar with. Globalization is the term we use to describe the process of the world becoming one, or, perhaps more accurately, the world increasing in the oneness that already exists. Whether it is the social, economic, political, religious, or environmental sphere that is in focus, all of human endeavor has come home to live in the context of this oneworld reality. One could argue that global humanity is the inescapable and logical conclusion to the history of mankind. It is the culmination of generations of human endeavor, expansion and interaction, even the plan of God.

Globalization describes the process. Oneworld defines the result. We are living in a new era of history. The paradigm of the oneworld era encompasses both process and result, within the context of the time in which we are now living. Oneworld precepts are all around us. We hear their message everyday, "One world. We are living in one world." Our lives are affected by oneworld dynamics—the price of gas rises and falls according to the global economy. The planet itself reels, or recovers, according to the collective stress put upon it by all the people in the world. The oneworld era even has a new method of war, called terrorism, which spreads around the globe like a virus in the host body.

The Anglican-Ism has come down through time and history to find itself intact in this new era. I say intact meaning continuing in existence; intact, yet not necessarily whole; poised, but not yet fully activated. It appears as a ready, if somewhat rough-hewn, vessel, and could rightly have great effect in our time. That is provided the Anglican Fellowship can first be set in order.

The Anglican-Ism is a global phenomenon. Since the Anglican Church has already spread around the world in the previous historical paradigms, it is now adapting naturally to global interaction. In many ways Anglicans have been functioning globally with each other for quite some time. Now that interaction is being expanded, as Anglicans are pressed to interact not only with each other, but also with the whole spectrum of church and society.

Paradigm to paradigm, the world has shifted, changed, morphed into new and different modes of being. The monarchial systems of the medieval time gave way to the Enlightenment, and the age of reason in the modern period. As modernity disintegrated into the postmodern period, reason was supplanted by experience as the defining sense of what it means to be human.

Now in the oneworld era experience has gone viral. Participation reigns as the new mode of being human. We find our identity through everything that we are participating in and with. Participation in all the world has to offer, and indeed, it is all on the table.

Oneworld Era

The two visions which began to come into focus in the postmodern era are each growing stronger and more distinct. If the oneworld paradigm is the ultimate melting pot, it is also the ultimate refiners fire. In the same way that the postmodern milieu radicalized the ideals of modernity, oneworld dynamics are radicalizing the postmodern theological and moral tenets. Inclusivity, tolerance, and pluralism which were previously amorphous ideals, have become concrete and are taking shape in the institutions and practices of oneworld life. Orthodoxy is being pressed upon from every side; called upon to defend its positions; clarify its stance; and articulate precisely the values and beliefs which are essential. Both visions are being melted. Both visions are being refined. As a result, both are emerging stronger and more clearly defined. The question is, "Which one will claim the prize—the soul of oneworld?"

The crisis has only just begun. Anglicans are the canary in the coal mine, gasping for air while worldwide Christianity looks on to see how much oxygen is left. Denial, reconciliation, and détente will not suffice. Reformation is the only way forward for the Christian church in the midst of oneworld. In order to survive, flourish, and proclaim the gospel, the church must become one as well. This is after all Jesus' prayer for us in John 17:21: "that they may all be one, just as you, Father, are in me, and I in you." The Reformation of the sixteenth century brought a splintering of Christianity. It was centrifugal in nature, spinning outward and separating the parts from the whole. The reformation required in the twenty-first century is just the opposite. It must be centripetal, pulling the pieces back from the periphery to make a cohesive whole.

Anglican Manifesto seeks to ignite this process of reformation. If *Manifesto* can become a catalyst for the Anglican Communion, then the Anglican-Ism can be effectively refined as a reagent ready to be poured into the oneworld context. The Anglican Church itself then becomes the catalyst, activating the various elements immersed in global Christianity. This will produce a chain reaction resulting in a transformation of the original elements. Of course, we should keep in mind that these types of chemical interactions usually produce some heat as a byproduct. This is to be expected and must be taken into account in the equation.

The sacramental principle derived from an enhanced understanding of the biblical/sacramental worldview provides a basis for unity within the body of Christ. In a way this principle is the centripetal force pulling the elements back together. Perhaps it has always been there, beneath the surface, exerting a counter effect to slow the fracturing, until now the process is being reversed. Slowly, the center begins to grow, gaining mass and size until tremendous forces fuse the fragments back together. The sacramental principle starts as an idea, a theology; a way of seeing which then becomes a way of being. It is likely being discerned already in many quarters of the Christian church.

Let us now consider further the composite makeup of the oneworld historical paradigm in which we are now living. For it is in this paradigm which we will see the completion of the two visions, and the emergence of the Oneworld Religion vs. the Oneworld Church. The process for unification in Christendom will also become evident through our discussion.

Composite of the Oneworld Era

Living in the new paradigm of oneworld means connectivity; the world is increasingly interconnected. By extension, the people in the world are increasingly connected, along with their thoughts, ideas, and expressions of faith. Social media connects individuals with family and friends, and with virtually anyone else who may share a common interest, in a virtual ocean of human relationship. The internet cables and satellites connect products and services with consumers, and now even make possible face to face interactions with businesses and governments alike. The whole world has gone digital. Perhaps in the end, it is the language of ones and zeros that accomplishes our commonality.

Let us consider once again the connections that comprise the structural components which hold the Oneworld paradigm together. How is the world joined together in one? What are the cords that bind us together? And, what are the values that promote and reinforce the new order of the day?

For the sake of brevity, what follows is a list of connections—physical, relational, and spiritual—that are readily observed in the present, and growing stronger every day. These are the cords that bind the global village together, and it is important to note that they do not function independently of one another, but are intertwined like a plate of spaghetti:

Oneworld Era

Connections

Digital	Internet; Satellite communications; Wireless; GPS
Transport	24-hr global travel; Overnight shipping around the world
Economic	Stocks; Commodities; Currencies; Manufacturing; Energy
Political	G20; Peace and War; United Nations; Trade Agreements
Religious	Interfaith Dialogue; United Religions Initiative; Syncretism
Personal	Facebook; eHarmony; Twitter; Instagram

The space which surrounds the globe is the most readily available means of connection for all the world. In many ways the oneworld era began when the first pictures of the planet were taken from outer space. It was then that the people of earth could see for themselves the oneworld in which we all live and participate. The international space station, manned by astronauts from many different nations, represents a kind of icon in the sky of oneworld. Now private space companies are moving to make this connection even more viable. You and I can go to space and see the oneworld for ourselves. Soon FedEx will deliver a package from Los Angeles to Hong Kong in a couple of hours, by sending it through the route of a commercial space rocket. People will be soon to follow. When you absolutely have to be on the other side of the world by noon, head for the nearest Spaceport. Of course the price of the ticket will be uber-class.

The reality of oneworld is nowhere more evident than in the commerce we now engage in across the globe. Goods and services are available from everywhere to everyone, in ways that would have staggered the imagination only a couple decades past. Corporations have risen that span the globe, operating in and beyond the mere realm of countries. Soon Amazon will have twenty-four hour delivery by drone. These economic engines are the driving force within a oneworld economy, and have themselves become icons which people recognize and participate in all around the globe. Following the tragedy of 9/11, and the destruction of the twin towers, a new complex was rebuilt. Out of the ashes of terrorism there has arisen an icon that symbolizes the resilience of human endeavor. The name for this symbol is the One World Trade Tower. This building has recently been certified as the tallest building in North America, a beacon of humanity joined together through worldwide trade.

One World Trade Tower

Icons of the Oneworld Era

Google

United Nations

The Dow

Facebook

Coca-Cola

McDonald's

Starbucks

Apple

Amazon

FedEx

As the globalization process accelerates, the oneworld era has developed and is exerting its own particular set of values, in order to complete and maintain the final result. In keeping with the new paradigm, these values are asserted to smooth out the anomalies in the system. Anomalies which left unassimilated result in friction, conflict, and constriction of global flow of ideas and commerce. Taken together these values and connections formulate the underlying principles of the paradigm, which mold and guide our thinking and actions in subtle ways that we are often unaware of.

Values

Instantivity	Instant communication; Instant information; Instant gratification
Technology	Cell phones; Networks; Fast computers; Xbox and Virtual Reality
Mobility	Personal travel and relocation; Resource availability everywhere
Opportunity	Wealth with unlimited restrictions and accountability
Pleasure	Freedom to participate in whatever we desire
Power	Freedom to take whatever we desire
Inclusivity	Pluralism; Relativism; Tolerance

Add the connections and values listed above, and the sum total equals the spirit of the age.

Once again, please take note how the values above all contribute to the goal of participation. We want to talk now, instantly participating in each other's lives—seeing the photos, sharing the moment, learning the immediate gossip. We want to feel the connection, knowing that we can partake of all the world offers at any given moment. Experiences that are beyond our reach in the physical world are now easily available through virtual reality. This alternate is becoming less virtual and more reality day by day. Taboos of human sexuality have disappeared into the instant gratification of online participation. Photos and movies are giving way to live performance video streamed into the privacy of the mind. Societal boundaries of death, murder, mayhem, and destruction, which in the past where fraught with risk of physical harm or prison, can now be enjoyed and experienced via the virtual gaming industry, with seemingly no consequences. And yet, what is the real consequence to the human soul?

Participation reigns supreme. It is the offer—the enticement. The cultural matrix of the oneworld paradigm is constantly beaming this message to us. These are the values that are important, participate in them. Here are the means available to you to make connections, use them. Look to the icons of the age, join with them in participation. Through participation you will find fulfillment. Participation is not only the way to achieve your goal, it is the goal. The human desire is to participate, and now we can do so instantly. Even beyond simple desire and availability, participation is at many levels required. We can no longer even be able to function in "normal" life, without our active participation in the dynamics of oneworld. How can we live without e-mails and texts? How can we find our way without the map icon on our cell phone? How will we find the nearest Starbucks? Make a transaction without a credit card? Or complete our college degree without online education? We are all participating in the new historical paradigm, and the values thereof, perhaps without even really thinking about it. After all this is the way paradigms function, beneath the surface of conscious awareness. That is unless we are willing to take the time for a more rigorous analysis.

These underlying principles and external pressures of the oneworld era also combine to exert their influence upon the realm of faith and religion. In a world that is being shrink wrapped tighter and tighter, the potential for religious conflict is readily evident. Major points of friction exist around the globe between Muslims and Christians, Jews, and Hindus. A host of minor frictions is also in place across the spectrum of religious practices. This conflict appears as a major anomaly which must be smoothed out or the whole system could come crashing down.

Oneworld Era

The Rise of the Tribes

As the world crunches closer together in its quest to become one, the sense of personal identity and belonging begins to dissipate. Oneworld is after all a big concept. How can a person find their place in it? In the face of such a behemoth, fear and loneliness are a natural response. The rise of the tribes is a natural byproduct, a counterweight to the leverage being applied to individual lives. Tribes are small. Tribes are mobile. They provide safety, support, and structure. Most importantly, tribes define roles clearly for their members. This kind of structure gives a sense of stability and a place to belong, a kind of island of solid ground in the midst of a oneworld ocean. In addition, tribes also provide a place to fulfill the desire for participation, thereby fulfilling the need of the current paradigm.

Tribes may be formed from many different criteria, and we are seeing their formation today. There are socioeconomic groups who have banded together for common benefit, purpose and interest. Political tribes of like-minded individuals seek to move their agenda forward on the oneworld stage. Sports tribes find identity and solidarity within the subculture of their team. Tribes may be generational, with gray hair or covered in tattoos, or even gang-like in expression. What they have in common is their identification with their own particular people group.

People groups are formed around common language, common geography, common beliefs, and common purpose. While simultaneously participating in the Oneworld paradigm, the tribes also pull aside to carve out space for their own. Ironically, the religions of the world are already very tribe-like in nature. This has become increasingly evident as the world fuses closer together in to one. Religions offer identity, belonging, and structure, a place where we know the rules and we are known by the rulers. They represent small spaces where people can participate in particular beliefs and values. At times these are in conflict with the spirit of the age, but increasingly that same spirit is moving its own beliefs and values into the tribes of religion to make them its own.

The church also fits easily into this motif. The various factions of Christianity provide an individual tribal identity in the midst of the whole of Christian expression. But, the more fractured a body becomes, the less ability it has to influence the greater events outside of itself. In contrast, the more unified a people group around a certain set of beliefs and values, the greater the ability to exert influence. This may sound like good news for the church, but as we shall see it is also prime opportunity for the counter movement toward the Oneworld Religion which resonates with the spirit of the age.

The theological foundation for this oneworld religion has already been laid. As we have discussed, monism and panentheism combine with inclusivity and pluralism to form the cornerstones of belief and practice. Socioeconomic and cultural values are exerting pressure to move the agenda forward. Religious leaders, seminaries, and organizations are actively promoting the vision. Soon the tribes will be viewed as threats. They need to be brought into the fold. The oneworld era will not tolerate these anomalies. Those who will not comply are not good for the whole.

In like manner, the Christian church, that is the faithful followers of Jesus who maintain the apostolic witness, will also be pressured to change, to conform, or to at least yield in the face of the good of the all. In order to maintain a consistent witness and be effective in the proclamation of the gospel, the church must come to terms with its own tribal qualities. Tribes of Presbyterians, Baptists, Evangelicals, Catholics, Orthodox, Pentecostal, Holiness, Bible Churches, Chapels and Vineyards of every flavor need to join together in faithfulness and prophetic witness in and to the oneworld era. The benefits of the tribes, personal identity, belonging, security and support, need not be lost. Instead, the threats we perceive from one another must be laid to rest. In truth, we actually have fellowship with each other in the deepest sense of the word. As Paul declares in his epistles, we are in Christ. It is this fellowship that we must recognize, promote, and celebrate, so that we may be one, and stand as one against an active and engaged Oneworld Religion which has a completely different agenda—the assimilation of all into an extreme humanism.

The intent of this thesis is to argue that in the oneworld era two emerging religious responses will become increasingly evident: the Oneworld Religion and the Oneworld Church. Oneworld Religion will further radicalize the pluralism of the postmodern age, gathering together the spectrum of all religious expressions under one banner. The Oneworld Church will consist of Christians who remain faithful to the faith once delivered, across the spectrum of Christian denominations. Then the work of *Anglican Manifesto* will be completed. And so, let us take a look at the following:

1. The compatibility and appeal of the emerging Oneworld Religion within the new paradigm
2. A descriptive portrayal of the Anglican Catalyst, with the practical applications of the Sacramental Principle

3. The effectiveness of a renewed Fellowship of Christian Churches in proclaiming the gospel to the next generation.

Oneworld Religion

The spirit of the age is pressing in upon the church: the Anglican Church, the Roman Catholic Church, Presbyterian, Methodist, Baptist, Orthodox, Evangelical, Pentecostal, independent, and every other church that upholds the faith once delivered to the saints. The crisis that has gripped Anglicans is prevalent throughout the other denominations, and non-denominations, as well. This is because it is the crisis of a paradigm shift, from which the churches must respond either proactively, or reactively. There is no middle ground. As we shall see, to remain passive is to be overrun, consumed, and subsumed into something fundamentally different.

Earlier, I posed the question, "Is it likely that the churches of the Christian faith will embrace a proactive response to the spirit of the age?" In answer, it remains possible, yet unlikely. If remaining passive is also not an option, then a reactive response will be the only other choice. This is what we are currently observing across the ecclesiastical landscape.

Church communities are forced into reaction. They are required to define exactly what they believe, and to decide which practices are acceptable and which are not. Boundaries must be set to protect the fertile ground of the kingdom—the holy ground of the hearts and minds of God's people. After all, we live in this age and we are constantly being bombarded with the messages of the age. When planted within us, these messages become weeds in the garden. If these weeds of worldly ideals are allowed to grow, eventually they will take over and choke out everything else.

In Borg-like fashion the spirit of the age does not obliterate that which it touches, instead it infuses it with new parts, and alters what is needed to adapt it to its own purposes. Wherever the theology, faith, and practice of an existing religious expression conforms to and enhances the new paradigm, it is embraced. Wherever theology, faith, and practice are in opposition, either directly or indirectly, they must be discounted, altered, or completely done away with, so as not to impede the "progress of humanity." In the case of the Christian faith and church, we must be assimilated. We must be infused with contemporary values and transformed into a new religious expression. One that is suited to the new paradigm—the Oneworld Religion. As stated previously in the chapter of the Two Visions, in order for

Anglican Manifesto

Christianity to fit it must be adapted, changed, altered so as not to offend by removing any claims of exclusivity, objective truth, or outdated morality.

Resistance is futile.

The emerging Oneworld Religion is a religion of harmony, syncretizing the common elements of all religious endeavors for the good of mankind. Inclusivity is rising as the preeminent value. As each worldwide or local community of faith becomes willing to include all others, each in turn are enriched by the deposit found elsewhere. Love and human goodness are the foundations upon which the New Temple stands, with portals opening in all directions. Remember God is in all, and all are in God. Thus, Hindu, Muslim, Christian, Jew, Baha'i, Sikh, Wiccan, and even Atheist, may experience a sense of the Divine within themselves. For it is commonly asserted by the spirit of the age that God, the universe, mankind, and the world are in fact One. So, all must move beyond the narrow dogmatism which breeds conflict and religious strife, and embrace a "faith for the world" which, incidentally, fulfills the values of the world.

The theological term for this is monism, from *mono*, or one. Monism unifies all religions by conceiving "God" as a divine force, or spirit, found within the universe. As such, "God" is available for everyone's participation, and the religions of the world are all means of connection. God is like a vast oilfield of energy lying beneath the surface. Religions are like oil wells that drill down to tap into the source. The wells may be constructed differently, may look and function distinctly from one another, but in actuality all are accomplishing the same thing with the same "God." Once we can reach this higher understanding, then the religious conflicts that threaten our oneworld can be resolved.

Oneworld Era

**All religions embraced as making a contribution
to the divine harmony of human existence, endeavor, and interaction.**[1]

The Oneworld Religion preached above is actively coming into being, even as we speak. Many Christian churches have already morphed into an enclave of this new reality. Many more are grappling with forces and pressures from within and without to yield, to change, to embrace this phenomena, which can be oh so appealing. Those who believe in the faith once delivered, those churches of genuine Christianity, have three options; proactive, reactive, and passive. To remain passive is to be taken over, probably sooner rather than later. A reactive stance may also lose out in the end, although it is possible, and indeed evident, that the more that pressure comes from the outside, the more the reaction in response may fuse the fellowships of Christianity into the Oneworld Church. *Anglican Manifesto* is advocating a proactive response.

Oneworld Church

We began our thesis with an examination of the Anglican-Ism, and how it developed and traversed down through the historical paradigm shifts.

---

1. See appendix 4, *Symbols of Oneworld Religion*.

Manifesto continued with a critical analysis of the current crisis within the Anglican Communion, presenting potential solutions that are designed to set a new Anglican Fellowship into position as a catalyst for the unity of the Christian church worldwide. A theological foundation for such unity has been articulated in the chapter on the Sacramental Principle.

We must now consider the practical application of these solutions and their interaction with the principles of the emerging new paradigm—the oneworld era. Why does the Anglican expression of the Christian faith hold the potential to become a catalyst? How can a Oneworld Church emerge in a unity of fellowship, especially since that goal has proved elusive for the past two thousand years? And, how will such a renewed fellowship of the Oneworld Church be in contrast and conflict with the global village and the Oneworld Religion?

In order to begin, we must turn back for a moment to the end of chapter one on the Anglican-Ism. There we concluded with the description of Anglican faith, which holds together the four vibrant expressions of Christianity into a quad. These expressions have the potential to balance and enhance one another. The catholic expression emphasizes sacraments and focuses worship around them. Evangelicals uphold the Scripture as paramount, and emphasize teaching and proclaiming the word. The liberal stream polarized around service and compassion as the essence of following the gospel. At present the liberal expression of the church has been subsumed into the spirit of the age. As noted in the last chapter, we should be careful not to lose the genuine liberal qualities embodied in Jesus himself: concern for the poor; care for the sick; compassion for the outcast and disenfranchised. Here we will reclaim the real liberal, defined as being within the boundaries of orthodoxy. Finally, the charismatic movements of modern and postmodern time periods renew our knowledge of the power and presence of God in our midst through the action of the Holy Spirit.

Oneworld Era

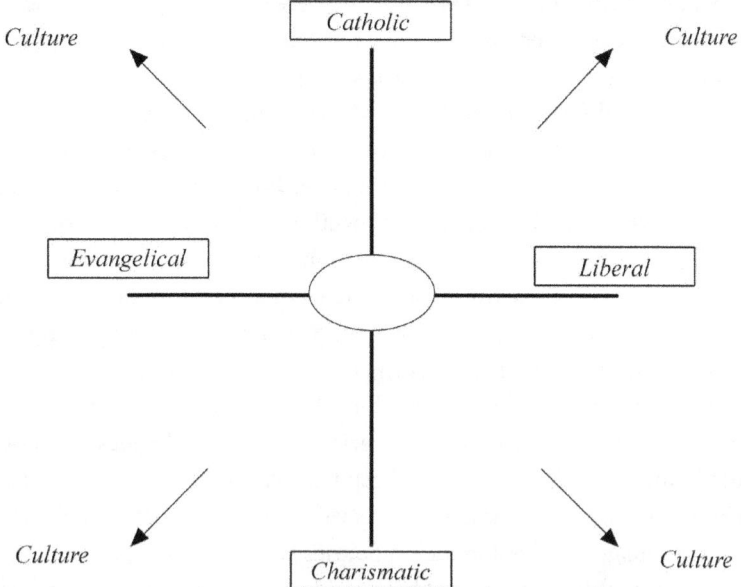

Above shows the four poles of Christianity derived from the historical streams of faith and practice, and brought together as a grid within Anglican-Ism

This fourfold grid, fomented through the pressure and time of the historical paradigm shifts, becomes the core molecular structure that binds the elements of the catalyst together. It is the base substance to which we add the additional elements to produce the catalytic reaction. Note: in chemistry when inert elements are mixed together they may simply remain passive and not bond with one another. But, when a catalyst is added, it becomes the missing connection that sets off a chain reaction creating a chemical bond—light and heat often occur as a result, and if one is not careful explosions are known to happen!

Let us now think of the greater expressions of Christianity as the various base elements. These are the historical streams of Catholic, Evangelical, Charismatic, and Real Liberal Christianity that have flowed down through time to the present. Mostly they exist separated from one another in church structures that emphasize the particular theological perspective of each one. Thus, they remain isolated within their own respective quadrants, like inert elements contained within their own beakers. The first step to produce bonding is to bring them close to one another, within the same vessel where they may touch and interact. This is precisely what has occurred by means of the Anglican Church. Catholic, Evangelical, Charismatic, and Real Liberal expressions of Christian faith and practice have been brought into close proximity with one another. All vibrant traditions of faith, albeit different from one another, have become accepted as valid parts of the whole.

Bringing the various streams of Christianity together is a beginning. Yet, each of these expressions may continue to remain essentially separate and distinct from one another, without ever bonding or fusing into something new, like oil and water shaken together in a jar quickly become separate from one another. In order for these four to fuse together and become something greater than the sum of their equal parts other key elements must be included, and contaminates must be prevented from being interjected into the mix. Let us format the mix one stage at a time.

First, in order to keep our efforts uncontaminated from the world around us, we must set clear boundaries around our Anglican prototype. These boundaries also function to keep the four poles of our core structure in close proximity with one another. As we discussed in chapter 5, the lack of clearly articulated and enforced boundaries within the Anglican-Ism is one of the main problems in need of being addressed. Anglican comprehensiveness allowed the four expressions to find a home together. Anglican openness facilitated the flow of the gospel outward to the culture. However, what is conspicuously absent in the illustration above are any boundaries that prevent the reversal of the flow—from the culture into the church. When the arrows are reversed, the culture imports the ideals of the spirit of the age into the life of the church. In a kind of backward prophetic witness, the church gets transformed to look and be more like the world. This is exactly what is happening with increasing intensity in the oneworld paradigm.

Therefore, in forming the basis for the Oneworld Church, we begin by bringing the historical streams together. The next essential step is to set the boundaries which must be in place to distinguish the church from the world. This distinction is an ontological reality, which means the church is different in its very being. We are in Christ, not of the world.

The boundaries that are necessary and proper include:

1. The Word of God—Holy Scripture
2. Basic interpretive principles
3. Creeds—expanded and explained
4. Biblical morality

These boundaries listed above are represented in the next illustration below by the circle drawn around the Quad. These boundaries effectively set a line between what can be considered Christian, and what cannot. The four expressions of the church are all contained within these bounds of Christian faith and practice—orthodoxy and orthopraxis. Yet, any one of them is vulnerable to embracing principles and practices which are aligned with the spirit of the age, pulling that part of the church beyond what can be considered as genuinely Christian. The proper boundaries of the church prevent the undo influence of values of the surrounding culture from coming in, but remain open for the influence of the church to flow out in prophetic witness.

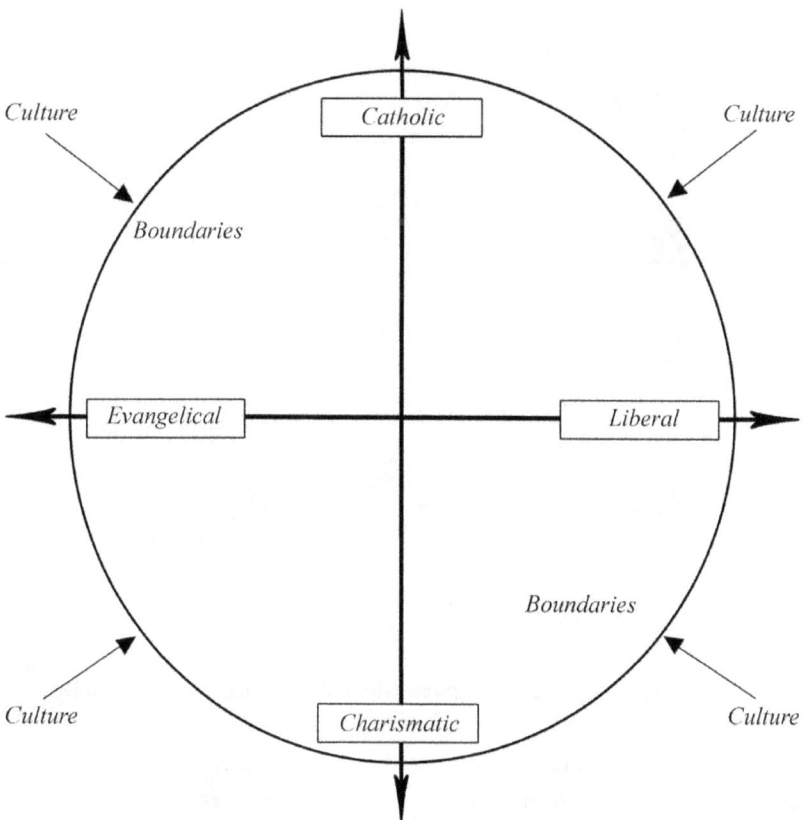

Circle around the quad represents the boundaries of orthodoxy
Each expression must remain within the bounds
to be considered part of the Christian church

Next, we shift our point of view to see not poles, which are separated from each other at a greater distance, but quadrants, sharing long lines of common points with one another. This gives a breakthrough from a change of perspective, as we come to realize that the central expressions of the Christian faith are not as isolated from one another as may be assumed. Even though each resides distinctively in its own quadrant, they share much in common at the central core and along the borders where they touch.

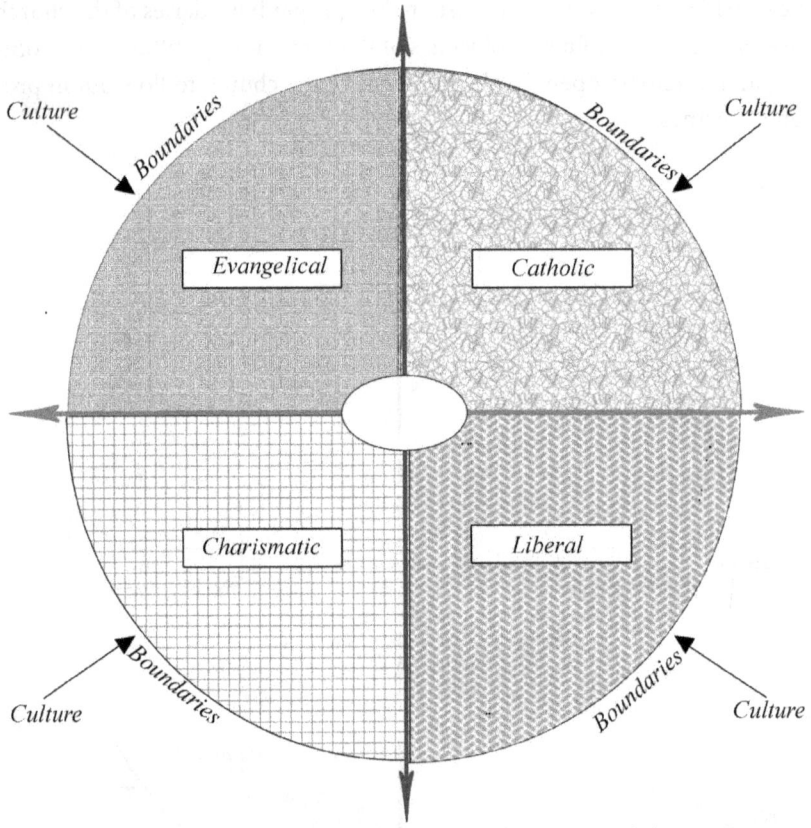

Expressions of faith form quadrants within the boundaries of Christianity

Since, each of the Church traditions emphasizes a particular vibrant expression of the faith, it is helpful to distill the essence of each. That is to say if each is distilled, what part does each contribute to the whole, the elixir, of the gospel:

Catholic = Sacrament

Liberal = Service

Evangelical = Scripture

Charismatic = Spirit

Oneworld Era

In fairness, elements from each quadrant, or church expression, often spill over and are found mixed within the others, to a greater or lesser degree. Yet, the churches of Christianity continue to remain distinct, and are not bonded with one another. Thus we must add the Sacramental Principle as the bonding agent, the final element in the mix.

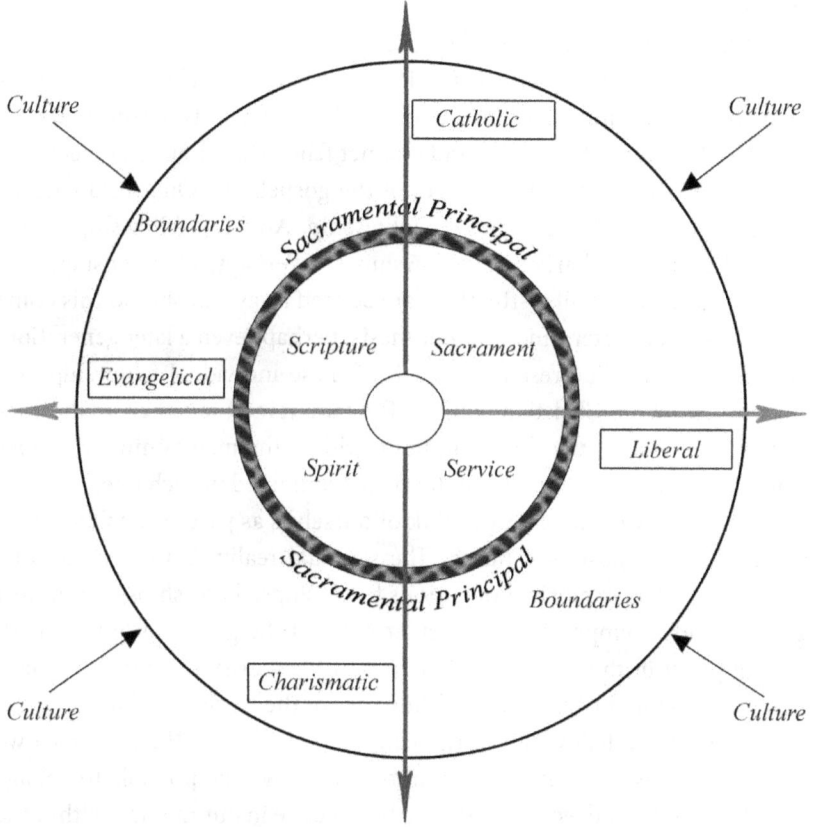

The illustration above shows how the Sacramental Principle is
present and active in every quadrant of Christian expression
This theological principle balances the transcendent and immanent qualities of God
and demonstrates how God manifests himself through
Sacrament, Scripture, Spirit, Service

Should the first stage of *Anglican Manifesto* be accomplished, and a new Anglican Fellowship emerge, this is what it will look like. This model would then become the catalyst, in and of itself, for the Christian churches worldwide. Imagine each quadrant of our diagram extending outward to cover all the different churches of that persuasion, keeping in mind that regardless of which quad they reside in, all must remain within our prescribed boundaries of distinctly Christian theology and practice. The Sacramental Principle is intertwined throughout all and affirming all as viable expressions of faith and practice. In such an understanding all expressions are bonded together and pulled to the center of common purpose and mutual respect.

The result is the Oneworld Church.

To be clear, what is being envisioned and promoted here is not necessarily oneworld church administration. Rather, it is a unity of common faith expressed through the various and distinct fellowships bonded together in the common pursuit and principles of the gospel. The Oneworld Church comprised of the Roman Catholic fellowship, Anglican fellowship, Evangelical fellowship, Charismatic fellowship, etc. Perhaps, a further stage may be envisioned when all distinctions are cleared away, but should this come to pass, it is for a later time, another thesis, perhaps even a later generation. Nevertheless, in the present day each of these individual fellowships are part of the whole Christian church. They are joined together by the Sacramental Principle, purified from the world by the maintaining of proper boundaries, and able to share of the riches contained in each one.

We simply must begin to think of ourselves as part of the One, Holy, Catholic, and Apostolic Church. The spiritual reality is that we are one church, which is comprised of various fellowships, fellowships that in turn give individual emphasis to particular parts of the gospel of Jesus Christ. I am a priest in the Anglican fellowship of the Christian church. Perhaps you are a member of the Baptist fellowship of the Christian church, or the Roman Catholic fellowship of the Christian church, or the . . . Once we have recognized the basis of our unity, then it will be possible to engage together as one, and work together to be effective in our mission within the oneworld era.

When this kind of identification and mutual respect take place, the Christian church will then be in a position to regain the ability to function as it did in the first centuries, through the meeting together in council. The context the church faced in the early centuries of the faith was not unlike that which we face today. The Roman Empire was a place of radical pluralism, which upheld values of power and pleasure. Emperors sought to bring the world together as one, at least the world that was known at the time. Major centers of Christianity existed that were separate and distinct from one another, and organized into the major sees with their respective bishops: Jerusalem, Alexandria, Antioch, Constantinople, and Rome. These were in fellowship with one another, and when the time arrived for consultation they would convene a council in which all were represented. Together they prayed, conferred and discerned the mind of Christ and the directions of the Holy Spirit.

The Oneworld Church has the opportunity to regain this conciliar model for life and vitality in our time. Representatives from the various streams of Christianity would be able to join together in council. The councils of the early church produced magnificent statements of faith such as the Nicene Creed. They affirmed the boundaries of Christian belief and protected the church from the heresies of the world. The councils maintained the common unity of all believers in Christ, and so strengthened the whole body. There is no reason why the councils of our own time could not do the same. In fact, they may be needed now more than ever.

What we have been describing so far might be considered a proactive model for the emergence of a unified church in the oneworld era. In order for this approach to be effective, it will require leadership, investment of time, energy, and communication, both within and between Christian churches. In short, it requires action. The action advocated by this *Anglican Manifesto*. Is this likely to happen? Will the churches contained with the various quadrants of our diagrams willingly acknowledge one another, and move toward mutual fellowship?

Only time will tell.

Conclusion

The tenets of modern liberal theology, with an emphasis on humanism, subjective authority, divine immanence, and social reform have come home to rest in the postmodern context. The guiding principles of the postmodern era—pluralism, relativism, tolerance and deconstructionism—have fused with liberal theology to produce a fresh theological vision. Under pressure from the growing realities of the global village, this vision has morphed into a new movement, with a new ideal: Oneworld Religion. A Religion in which a revised pseudo-Christianity finds its place subordinated within the circle of religious thoughts and practices.

A neo-humanism has arisen in the world, which promotes the idea that all are inherently good, or even divine. This increasingly popular viewpoint cannot be reconciled with classical Christian belief in a holy and transcendent God to whom all must give account. Subjective authority derived from the personal experience of the self is in direct opposition with objective authority maintained in the Holy Scripture for all people in every generation. And so the conflict has arisen, and the crisis has begun to come to age as we move into the oneworld era.

While living in the same historical context, much of the Christian church retains a commitment to the faith once delivered to saints. Across denominational lines, the "orthodox" hold fast to the belief in an objective authority of the Bible and the need for regeneration of sinful human nature. Rather than being informed by the prevailing cultural values, many Anglicans, Catholics, and Protestants continue to teach and confess the traditional principles and theology which have been the bedrock of the faith for two thousand years:

An exclusive view of Jesus as the means of salvation for all mankind

The inspiration and authority of the Bible in all matters of faith and morality

The holy and transcendent nature of God

The need for divine grace to redeem and transform our humanity

The prophetic witness of the church to the world in all times and places

The conservatism portrayed above stands in stark opposition to the popular revisionism of the spirit of the age. Whereas the connections and values of the present historical paradigm are on track to produce a homogenous Oneworld Religion, so too the reassertion of the essentials of orthodoxy has the potential to bring into being a Oneworld Church. The emerging Oneworld Religion will stand in diametric opposition to a reunified Oneworld Church. This is because each maintains a commitment to a core set of beliefs and practices that are at heart irreconcilable.

The two visions are already present and well represented in the controversies of the Anglican Communion. In this thesis, I have sought to further explore the dynamics that have brought us to this historical juncture and continue to drive us forward into the future. As an orthodox Anglican priest, I see clearly the possibility for the Anglican reformation to become a worldwide reformation of the Christian church—one that would reunite Christendom in a way not seen since the early church. I believe the calling of the Anglican reformers of the twenty-first century goes far beyond just setting their own house in order, although this must be the first order of business. Rather, theirs is a calling to ignite the One Church movement worldwide.

Anglicanism is uniquely situated at this point in history to be the catalyst for this transformation of Christian expressions. Yet, consider also the great danger and pitfalls to all concerned, in the church and in the world, should we not recognize the opportunity of this moment and fail to act. Christianity itself may well be subsumed in the coming tsunami of the Oneworld Religion.

The purpose of *Anglican Manifesto,* as stated from the beginning, is to formulate a statement of beliefs and principles, or values, with the intention of inciting action. It is a proactive faith and practice which I desire to incite—first within my own Anglican Church and then by extension to Christendom in general. A revived and restructured fellowship of Anglican Churches could readily become a model and a catalyst for the reformation of the various Christian Fellowships worldwide.

Utilizing the Sacramental Principle as the theological means of recognizing and affirming vibrant expressions of faith that are often separated among the streams of Christianity, we have the potential to move together as fellowships united in a Oneworld Church. As such, we will be ready and able to proclaim the gospel in the oneworld era.

In direct opposition stands the emerging Oneworld Religion. It seeks to captivate the hearts and minds of our generation and the generation to come. Which movement will succeed? The Church as the people of God, who stand firm in the faith once delivered, or the harmony of religion with its offer of love, inclusion, and liberality in union with the Divine? In no small part the answer will be determined by you, the reader of this thesis.

> May God our Father
> Who brought again our Lord Jesus Christ from the dead
> Strengthen you in every good work
> To fulfill his purposes, through Jesus Christ our Lord. Amen

Appendix 1

The Chicago-Lambeth Quadrilateral 1886, 1888

Adopted by the House of Bishops
Chicago, 1886

We, Bishops of the Protestant Episcopal Church in the United States of America, in Council assembled as Bishops in the Church of God, do hereby solemnly declare to all whom it may concern, and especially to our fellow-Christians of the different Communions in this land, who, in their several spheres, have contended for the religion of Christ:

1. Our earnest desire that the Saviour's prayer, "That we all may be one," may, in its deepest and truest sense, be speedily fulfilled;

2. That we believe that all who have been duly baptized with water, in the name of the Father, and of the Son, and of the Holy Ghost, are members of the Holy Catholic Church;

3. That in all things of human ordering or human choice, relating to modes of worship and discipline, or to traditional customs, this Church is ready in the spirit of love and humility to forego all preferences of her own;

4. That this Church does not seek to absorb other Communions, but rather, co-operating with them on the basis of a common Faith and Order, to discountenance schism, to heal the wounds of the Body of Christ, and to promote the charity which is the chief of Christian graces and the visible manifestation of Christ to the world;

But furthermore, we do hereby affirm that the Christian unity ... can be restored only by the return of all Christian communions to the principles of unity exemplified by the undivided Catholic Church during the first ages of its existence, which principles we believe to be the substantial deposit of Christian Faith and Order committed by Christ and his Apostles to the Church unto the end of the world, and therefore incapable of compromise or surrender by those who have been ordained to be its stewards and trustees for the common and equal benefit of all men. As inherent parts of this sacred deposit, and therefore as essential to the restoration of unity among the divided branches of Christendom, we account the following, to wit:

1. The Holy Scriptures of the Old and New Testament as the revealed Word of God.
2. The Nicene Creed as the sufficient statement of the Christian Faith.
3. The two Sacraments,--Baptism and the Supper of the Lord,--ministered with unfailing use of Christ's words of institution and of the elements ordained by Him.
4. The Historic Episcopate, locally adapted in the methods of its administration to the varying needs of the nations and peoples called of God into the unity of His Church.

Furthermore, Deeply grieved by the sad divisions which affect the Christian Church in our own land, we hereby declare our desire and readiness, so soon as there shall be any authorized response to this Declaration, to enter into brotherly conference with all or any Christian Bodies seeking the restoration of the organic unity of the Church, with a view to the earnest study of the conditions under which so priceless a blessing might happily be brought to pass.

Note: While the above form of the Quadrilateral was adopted by the House of Bishops, it was not enacted by the House of Deputies, but rather incorporated in a general plan referred for study and action to a newly created Joint Commission on Christian Reunion.

Lambeth Conference of 1888
Resolution II

That, in the opinion of this Conference, the following Articles supply a basis on which approach may be by God's blessing made towards Home Reunion:

The Chicago-Lambeth Quadrilateral 1886, 1888

A. The Holy Scriptures of the Old and New Testaments, as "containing all things necessary to salvation," and as being the rule and ultimate standard of faith.

B. The Apostles' Creed, as the Baptismal Symbol; and the Nicene Creed, as the sufficient statement of the Christian faith.

C. The two Sacraments ordained by Christ Himself--Baptism and the Supper of the Lord ministered with unfailing use of Christ's words of Institution, and of the elements ordained by Him.

D. The Historic Episcopate, locally adapted in the methods of its administration to the varying needs of the nations and peoples called of God into the Unity of His Church.

Appendix 2
Anglican-Ism Terms and Characters

Thomas Wolsey: An ambitious colleague of King Henry VIII who rose in power to the rank of cardinal and papal legate over all the English bishops. Wolsey asserted his power in all walks of society, and supported the cause of education. However, Wolsey's exercise of power fostered "antipapalism and anticlericalism." Eventually he ran into conflict with Henry over the divorce of Katherine, and was charged with treason, but died before trial.

King Henry VIII: Bold, ambitious, audacious king of England. Henry ruled through the power of persuasion and ingenuity, utilizing the Parliament to pass laws against those who opposed his will, and convincing the populace that he had their best interests at heart. Henry facilitated the breach with Rome in order to secure his divorce from Katherine and subsequent remarriage to Ann Boleyn, naming himself as "Protector and Supreme Head of the English Church and Clergy." He magnified the office of archbishop of Canterbury and appointed Thomas Cranmer to the position. He dissolved the monasteries which had been a central feature of English Christianity for hundreds of years, to appropriate their income for the crown. Henry VIII remained ostensibly Catholic in doctrine, but may have had affinity for the growing reform movement. He revolutionized the constitution of the Church of England and effectively severed its subordination to Rome.

William Tyndale: As the ideas of the Reformers gained influence in the early 1500s the demand for an English Bible increased. William Tyndale took up the task of printing and distributing copies of the Bible in English. Forced to flee to Germany he continued his work smuggling the Bible to England in bales of wool. His addition of Protestant commentary to the Scripture eventually resulted in his death—condemned as a heretic.

Anglican-Ism Terms and Characters

Thomas Cranmer: The reform-minded archbishop of Canterbury during the reign of Henry VIII. Cranmer sought to unify the worship in the Church of England, and produced the Book of Common Prayer. The BCP retained elements of both Catholic and Protestant theology, rejoicing the moderates but drawing criticism from conservatives (Catholic) and Reformers (Protestant). Under Edward VI, Cranmer solidified his reformed views, so that when Mary became queen, and initiated the Catholic revival, he was tried and executed as a heretic.

The English Prayer Books (1459, 1552): Known as the Book of Common prayer, they were written and published by Thomas Cranmer. The prayer books sought to bring liturgical reform and continuity of worship to the English Church. Just prior to their publication a wide variety of worship expressions could be found, some severely lacking in content. The first prayer book retained much of the Catholic Sarum Rite, while the second, under Reformation influence, made significant changes to affirm protestant doctrines—especially regarding the nature of the Eucharist.

Mary Tudor: Ascended to the throne of England upon Edward VI's death in 1553. Mary was a devout Catholic who had lived for twenty years in exile in France. She immediately set out to undo the breach with Rome, and nullified the enactments of Henry VIII. Mary nearly succeeded in returning England to the Roman Catholic fold, but her marriage to the king of Spain, and the spirit of nationalism and reform already part of English life, caused her to fail.

Elizabethan Settlement: The reestablishment of the Church of England by Elizabeth as a distinct body apart from Rome. Elizabeth reversed the policy of Mary, who sought to return the church to papal oversight, and charted a Via Media, which retained catholic polity while affirming protestant reforms—especially communion in both kinds and married clergy. The settlement asserted the queen as "Supreme Governor" of the English Church.

John Jewel's Apology: Argued in favor of the Elizabethan Settlement. Jewel appealed to Scripture and the early church, asserting that the Church of England was truly catholic. His arguments for England and against Rome were published in *Apologia pro ecclesia Anglicana*.

Richard Hooker's Laws of Ecclesiastical Polity: Hooker was educated by John Jewel, and continued the intellectual work of establishing the Anglican Church. Hooker "sought to provide Anglicanism with a philosophical and logical basis" in his book, *On the Laws of Ecclesiastical Polity*. He refutes a growing Puritan influence in England, which asserted that Scripture is the only test of what is correct. Hooker believed that the Church could make laws as long as they did not contradict Scripture.

William Laud: Chancellor and archbishop under Charles I (1629–1640), whose passion for reform often bordered on severe. Laud was closely aligned with the king, and asserted his power against all manner of irregularities in the church. He sought to unify the church by means of strict enforcement of the law, and saw himself as "born to set other people right." He demanded obedience to the BCP by the bishops, and used the courts to enforce his authority.

The Caroline Divines: A group of writers and scholars who continued in the tradition of Jewel and Hooker. They sought to provide to the world a viable description of the Anglican Church, thus establishing an intellectual basis for the life of the church. In particular they sought to ground the Church of England in the tradition of the early church apart from Rome, maintaining its catholic nature and witness to the apostolic faith: Lancelot Andrews, George Herbert, John Cosin, Jeremy Taylor, Nicholas Ferrar.

Oliver Cromwell: The Puritan member of the House of Commons, who became master of England. Cromwell formed a cavalry after civil war broke out in 1642, and quickly defeated troops loyal to the king. After the king was defeated, Cromwell took the reins of power as Lord Protectorate and set about religious reforms that sought to make room for "Presbyterians, Baptists, Independents, and even some moderate advocates of episcopacy." He attempted to make England into a republic, but failed to do so in the end.

Cambridge Platonists: A group of scholars primarily members of Emmanuel College, a center of the Puritan community, who appealed to reason as the deliberator of religious strife. They sought to find harmony between philosophy and religion, and espoused a mystical spirituality devoted to prayer and meditation. They sought after a pure and holy life, and the reconciliation of all truth with the Spirit of God.

Latitudinarians: Originally a term for the Cambridge Platonist, it was later applied to those who succeeded them. A school of liberal, rational men who deplored the religious enthusiasm of their times and sought to use reason as a means of attaining a quiet ordered society. They set high standards of morality and charity, devoting themselves to good works and tolerance of other Christians.

Non-Jurors: A group of about four hundred clergy who refused to acknowledge the appointment of William and Mary as sovereigns over England. The Non-Jurors believed strongly in the Divine Rite of Kings. Therefore, when James II was deposed, yet remained alive, they would not compromise their loyalty for conscience sake. This resulted in their deprivation, and schisms in the church when their offices were reappointed.

The SPCK and SPG: Two religious societies formed in 1698 and 1701, respectively, devoted to the spread of the gospel and the work of the church overseas. The Society for Promoting Christian Knowledge provided religious literature abroad, and founded libraries and schools. The Society for the Propagation of the Gospel sought to establish the church in the colonies and convert the native peoples.

Deism: A religious philosophy based upon nature and reason. Deists retained God as the original Creator, but removed all involvement on his part after the finished work. Special revelation—i.e., the work of Christ—was ignored in favor of a non-demanding faith in reason and the understandability of the universe.

John Wesley: Anglican priest who, following an unsuccessful mission to Georgia, was converted through an encounter with God at a Moravian Pietist gathering on Alderstreet. During the reading of Paul's Epistle to the Romans, Wesley felt his heart "strangely warmed" and recognized God's personal gift of salvation through Jesus Christ. Wesley preached this "New Birth" experience all over England, often outdoors to the masses with dramatic results. His follow up Bible study groups became known as the Methodist movement.

George Whitfield: A contemporary of Wesley dubbed the Divine Dramatist. Early in life Whitfield studied to be an actor, but upon his conversion set out to preach the gospel. He traveled to America and preached with astonishing results up and down the Atlantic seaboard. A gifted and powerful orator, he preached in the open air to crowds numbering into the thousands. Thus, he initiated the first Great Awakening in American history.

John Henry Newman: Leader of the Oxford Movement, a group of scholars who sought to reform the church from without. Newman wrote tracts exhorting a return to catholicity, especially that of the early church fathers. In Protestant England, Newman and the Tractarians met much resistance for their dislike of the Reformers, and advocation of Roman Catholic doctrine. Eventually, Newman left the Church of England and became a Catholic himself.

F. D. Maurice (1805–1872): An early modern scholar who was brought up as a Unitarian, but ordained in the Church of England. His teachings were rationalistic, pantheistic, and anti-dogmatic. He believed that God's revelation meant the unveiling of his nature by degrees, and that everlasting punishment referred to punishment administered in eternity not lasting forever.

The Lambeth Conferences: Anglican General Council of Bishops, begun in 1867. In the nineteenth century worldwide growth of the Anglican Communion presented problems that needed to be addressed. The success of the early conferences in defining the unity of the church, and addressing its concerns, led to regular conferences thereafter. They provide opportunity for decisions on church polity and theology, as well as fellowship between bishops. Lambeth magnified the office of archbishop of Canterbury.

Lux Mundi: A volume of theological essays published in 1889, written by clergy in favor of the Labor Movement. The essays were intended to provide a justification of Christian Socialism. This resulted in the formation of the Christian Social Union which worked for brotherhood and justice for all men.

Edinburgh Conference: An interdenominational gathering of missionaries and mission agencies in 1910. The conference fostered cooperation on the mission field, and addressed problems pertaining to such. From this gathering the Ecumenical movement was born, facilitating greater cooperation amongst various denominations.

William Temple: Archbishop of Canterbury 1942. Temple was involved in the birth of the Ecumenical movement, which lead to the formation of the World Council of Churches.

Arthur Michael Ramsey: Ordained archbishop of Canterbury in 1961. He was confronted with growing administrative burdens in the church along with rapid changes. Ramsey presided at Lambeth 1968 and had earlier met with the pope to initiate a dialogue toward full communion.

Appendix 3
Spiritual Pride

I am of Paul; I am of Apollo . . .

—1 CORINTHIANS 1:12

PRIDE MAY BE AT the root of all sin. Through pride Satan rebelled. Through pride Adam and Eve fell. As American Christians we live with the tension of cultural conditioning toward pride and achievement alongside the commands of Jesus that call for a humble spirit and a contrite heart. Often we recognize sinful pride, when it rears its head in materialism, arrogance, or the abuse of power in the secular realm. Yet, we are often less aware of pride when it comes disguised as spiritual endeavor.

"I am of Paul . . . I am of Apollo," spiritual pride comes in many forms. There is the pride of personality seen in the exaltation of the charismatic pastor or priest, someone who has achieved spiritual success, usually demonstrated by a large congregation with lots of money. This leader may be afflicted with spiritual pride, and/or the congregation, as well: our church is the biggest church; our church is the one with the right doctrine; we are most like the early church; the most loving, most holy, best teaching, best healing; we teach the Bible; we speak in tongues; we have been around the longest; we do the liturgy the right way.

In the present Anglican context, spiritual pride has the potential to become one of the most dangerous impediments to reformation and revival. As stated earlier, orthodox Anglicans need to get on with reclaiming the foundations of the Christian faith, and then build into the next paradigm. However, as we live through the "long slow train wreck" of the Anglican

Spiritual Pride

Communion, instead of a unified and vibrant new fellowship, we face the danger of plethora of provinces, dioceses, parishes, and self-proclaimed Anglican groups and groupies.

The opportunity for spiritual pride is ripe. The longer the orthodox Anglicans remain huddled in their own particular splinter groups, the greater the possibility of spiritual pride. It is only natural to be invested in our own group and position, and to begin to derive our identity from ourselves. However, before we look to those "other groups," perhaps we best start with our own. First and foremost we must recognize that we are followers of Jesus and our identity is found only in him.

Spiritual pride will destroy revival if we let it, because it will prevent the unification that is required, all the while convincing us that our way is the right way. This is not to say that we must not distinguish between truth and error, between right doctrine and heresy, between what is moral or immoral. These we are called to as a matter of discernment. Unity is based in truth and agreement to that truth. The truth of Christ found in the Holy Scripture must become the touchstone of our identity, and the foundation of our common life.

Appendix 4
Symbols of Oneworld Religion

Comparison of Premodern, Modern, and Postmodern Views/Situation
Larry Kirkpatrick, HANDOUT, presentation 3, Northeast Washington Camp Meeting 2013-07-25, Sheridan Meadows, WA

	Premodern	Modern	Postmodern
1. **Starting Point**	God is beginning of all knowledge	*Knowing begins with the self.* "I think therefore I am"	Knowing begins with "I" *but there are seven billion "I"s,* all different
2. **Foundations**	Some foundationalism. Knowledge can be based on self evident truths needing no support from religion or other external authority	Profoundly foundationalist	Profoundly suspicious of all foundationalism. Sees these "foundations" as mere products of finite human beings
3. **Method**	Some method	Rigorously controlled method	There are methods, but insists on many. There are many ways, none producing truer results than others
4. **Objective knowledge**	Obtainable and desirable	Obtainable and desirable	Objective knowledge is neither attainable nor desirable. This view is seen to be a very positive development
5. **Universality of Truth**	"Truth" transcends the historical and is universally true	"Truth" transcends the historical and is universally true	"Truth" does *not* transcend the historical nor is universal. All truth claims are only true for *some* people in *some* times in *some* places
6. **Universe Open or Closed**	Universe is "open." Rigorous scientific relationships and understandings not worked out. God can operate via magic or science, a variety of means	Philosophical naturalism (becomes "science"). Matter, energy, time, space worked out. This is all that is. Leads to a "closed" universe with no God	"*Open*" to many methods. Less rigorous. Mystical appeals, pantheism, non-exclusive religious appeals, even superstition is acceptable
7. **Authority**	In the church	In the state and in self's reason	In the self and in experience (*not in* any group or other entity)
8. **Community**	Local, congregation/church-centric	Incidental and generic. Changing and rearranging, re-sorting	Personal inner circle/also virtual (internet). Personal and impersonal
9. **Personal Roles**	Traditional	Traditional roles (e.g., providing, protecting, judging, fathering, mothering, educating) absorbed by state	Roles are determined by *personal preference.* Education shift towards autodidacticism (self-teaching)

NOTES: -- Similar squares highlighted to show similarities. In some cases, Premodern, Modern, and Postmodern columns all quite different.
-- Chart created and adapted based esp. on D.A. Carson, *Becoming Conversant With the Emerging Church* (2005), pp. 87-98.

Casejustin / Dreamstime.com

All World Religion is One Religion

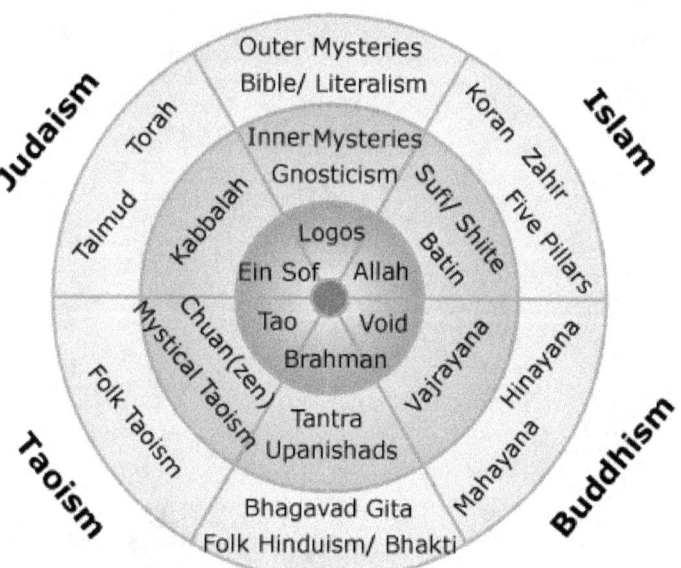

Scarboro Missions

Bibliography

Barth, Karl. *Church Dogmatics*. 14 vols. Edinburgh: T. & T. Clark, 1961.
Bloesch, Donald. *Toward a Theology of Word*. Downers Grove: InterVarsity, 1992.
Book of Common Prayer (BCP). New York: Church Hymnal Corporation, 1979.
Brooks, Peter Newman. *Thomas Cranmer's Doctrine of the Eucharist*. London: Macmillan, 1992.
Chadwick, Owen. *The Mind of the Oxford Movement*. Stanford: Stanford University Press, 1967.
Chan, Simon. *Spiritual Theology*. Downers Grove: InterVarsity, 1998.
Duffy, Eamon. *The Stripping of the Altars*. New Haven: Yale University Press, 1992.
Fairfield, Les. *Lecture on Richard Hooker*. Ambridge, PA: Trinity Episcopal School for Ministry, 2001.
Foster, Richard. *Streams of Living Water*. San Francisco: HarperCollins, 1998.
Gonzalez, Justo L. *The Story of Christianity*. Vol. 2. San Francisco: HarperCollins, 1985.
Grenz, Stanley J., and Roger E. Olson. *20th Century Theology*. Downers Grove: InterVarsity, 1992.
Jewel, John. *An Apology of the Church of England*. New York: Cornell University Press, 1963.
Lewis, C. S. *Mere Christianity*. New York: HarperCollins, 1980.
McFague, Sallie. *Models for God*. Minneapolis: Fortress, 1987.
McGrath, Alister. "Evangelical Distinctives." Chapter 2 of *Evangelicalism and the Future of Christianity*. Downers Grove: InterVarsity, 1995.
Moorman, John. *A History of the Church of England*. London: Black, 1976.
Niebuhr, H. Richard. *The Kingdom of God in America*. Middleton, CT: Wesleyan University Press, 1988.
Parsons, Donald J. "Some Theological and Pastoral Implications of Confirmation." Chapter 4 of *Confirmation Re-examined*, edited by Kendig Brubaker Cully. Wilton, CT: Morehouse-Barlow, 1982.
Payne, Leanne. *The Healing Presence*. Grand Rapids: Baker, 1989.
Robinson, John A. T. *Honest to God*. London: SCM, 1963.
Schleiermacher, Friedrich. *Speeches on Religion to Its Cultured Despisers*. Cambridge: Cambridge University Press, 1988.
Stott, John. "The Evangelical Doctrine of Baptism." Chapter 7 of *The Anglican Synthesis: Essays by Catholics and Evangelicals*, edited by W. R. F. Browning. Derby, UK: Smith, 1967.
Sykes, Stephen, et al., eds. *The Study of Anglicanism*. Minneapolis: Fortress, 1998.

Bibliography

Wainwright, Geoffrey. *Christian Initiation*. Chapter 3, "Initiation Medieval and Western." Richmond, VA: John Knox, 1969.

Wesley, John. "I Felt My Heart Strangely Warmed." In the *Journal of John Wesley*. Christian Classics Ethereal Library. http://www.ccel.org/ccel/wesley/journal.vi.ii.xvi.html.

Willard, Dallas. *The Divine Conspiracy*. San Francisco: HarperSanFrancisco, 1998.

Wright, N. T. *What St. Paul Really Said*. Grand Rapids: Eerdmans, 1997.

Yates, Arthur S. *Why Baptize Infants?* Norwich: Canterbury, 1993.

www.ingramcontent.com/pod-product-compliance
Lightning Source LLC
Chambersburg PA
CBHW071450150426
43191CB00008B/1291